NEW SERIES • VOLUME XXIV

COSTERUS

Rodopi

AMSTERDAM 1980

THE DISAPPEARANCE OF LITERATURE

by

Carol Johnson

Printed in the Netherlands
ISBN: 90–6203–761–5

To
Eileen, Colin and Roger
and
In honor of
Finella, Melusina, Goldberg and Bronwen
loyal non-readers, living and dead.

ACKNOWLEDGEMENTS

These essays first appeared in *Art International* and *Lugano Review* at the invitation of James Fitzsimmons whose suggestion that they be collected in a book I am now tardily following. An earlier version of "John Berryman: The Dream Songs" appeared in *The Harvard Advocate* (Vol. CIII. Number 1, Spring 1969). I am grateful as well to the Canada Council for a Leave Fellowship.

CONTENTS

Chapter One

THE DISAPPEARANCE OF LITERATURE

In an essay entitled "The Conquest of Ubiquity", Paul Valéry wrote:

> Our fine arts were developed, their types and uses were established, in times very different from the present, by men whose power of action upon things was insignificant in comparison with ours. But the amazing growth of our techniques, the adaptability and precision they have attained, the ideas and habits they are creating, make it a certainty that profound changes are impending in the ancient craft of the Beautiful. In all the arts there is a physical component which can no longer remain unaffected by our modern knowledge and power. For the last twenty years neither matter nor space nor time has been what it was from time immemorial. We must expect great innovations to transform the entire technique of the arts, thereby affecting artistic invention itself and perhaps even bringing about an amazing change in our very notion of art. 1

The innovations which Valéry anticipated have most conspicuously affected the transmission of visual images. The art of photography, the cinema developed their own language in precocious infancy, producing imaginative technical advances in arguably greater profusion and significance than those to which world literature of a comparable period can lay claim from its rhetorical resources. Indeed, literature sustains itself by borrowing from the other arts. Poetry renews its affiliations with music, making possible the *Cantos* of Pound, the *Four Quartets* of Eliot. In like manner architecture, cubism, impressionism, pointillism, the montage of cinematography have all lent themselves to literary uses, incomparably enriching the period we like to call modern. It was Eliot, that most conservative among the moderns, who called our attention to the permanent alteration to the rhythms of our poetry brought about by the invention of the internal combustion engine. Photography and the moving picture are products of an even more refined industrial process. Crucial to the effectiveness of film's influence on literature is film's ability to be more literal than words while remaining capable of symbolic statement. Moreover, space and time attain a more dynamic relation in film, a dynamic the verbal medium can approximate only in illusory terms. Arnold Hauser, whose discussion of naturalism, impressionism and the film age in the fourth volume of his *The Social History Of Art* so memorably encompasses this period, comments upon the complex interrelationship of space and time in film:

> . . . . as if space and time in film were interrelated by being interchangeable, the temporal relationships acquire an almost spatial character, just as space acquires a topical interest and takes on temporal characteristics, in other words a certain element of freedom is introduced into the succession of their moments. In the temporal medium of film we move in a way that is otherwise peculiar to space . . . proceeding from one phase of time into another. just as one goes from one room to another, disconnecting the individual stages in the development of events and grouping them, generally speaking, to the principles of spatial order. 2

Structures of recurrence and parallelism provide the coordinates which organize poetry. Gerard Manley Hopkins in a student paper written in 1865, ranging from the parallelisms of Hebrew poetry, the antiphons of Church music, to Greek, Italian and English poetic practice, isolated only two kinds of parallelisms: that wherein the opposition is clearly marked and that where opposition is transitional or chromatic. The various efforts of Pound, Dr. Williams, Wallace Stevens or Allen Ginsberg to "make it new" all have these constituents in common. Yet the more successful the poet is in intensifying the spatial and temporal properties of language, the more seamless his web, the more limited and specialized his audience becomes. Few, these days, are prepared to appreciate:

Twenty men crossing a bridge,
Into a village,
Are twenty men crossing twenty bridges,
Into twenty villages,
Or one man
Crossing a single bridge into a village.

Stevens, *"Metaphors of a Magnifico"*

or

Dung will not soil the slowworm's
mosaic. Breathless lark
drops to nest in sodden trash;
Drudge at the mallet, the may is down,
fog on fells. Guilty of spring
and spring's ending
amputated years ache after
the bull is beef, love a convenience.
It is easier to die than to remember.
Name and date
split in soft slate
a few months obliterate.

Bunting, *"Briggflatts"*

Whereas *Franju's Le Sang des Betes* or Resnais' *Nuit et Brouillard,* if they have circulated chiefly in art theatres, have done so not because their subtly articulated thesis - antithesis - synthesis can have been too abstruse for a general audience to comprehend, but because on the contrary their impact is too immediate, too profound and too troubling to be readily tolerable in commercial terms.

As for narrative prose, while it exhibits mastery of a range of filmic techniques from the relatively primitive flashback to the refinements of stream of consciousness, such mastery has been achieved at the cost of readers who are less and less willing to submit to the intensified demands of a seemingly atomized and diffuse subtext. Readers who resist surrendering to Virginia Woolf's vision of life as "a luminous halo, a semi-transparent envelope surrounding us from the beginning of consciousness to the end," who find her notion of the novelist's task "to convey this varying, this unknown and uncircumscribed spirit, whatever aberration or complexity it may display, with as little mixture of the alien and external as possible" a minimal inducement to persevere in reading *The Waves* - - readers who are hostile to or impatient with Joyce's *Ulysses* or *Finnegan's Wake* are quite possibly the same persons who respond with rapt and intransitive attention to Fellini's *8½* or Resnais' *Last Year in Marienbad*. Indeed, those who are able to summon only indifference for the New Novel of Robbe-Grillet may well be captivated by the hypnogogic images of *L'Imortelle*.

Valéry in 1928 permitted himself to doubt whether "what we call literature is to have a future." He speculated that perhaps "language will be replaced by other ways of reaching people's sensibility and intelligence," whether "a vast purely oral literature will not very shortly replace the written literature familiar to us," whether, in short, "literature as we know it may become an art as archaic and remote from every day life as geomancy or heraldry or falconry is today." And in support of this hypothesis he observed in the evolution of literature "an art founded on the abuse of language, on language as a creator of illusions as opposed to language as a transmitter of realities.3

Even if he wrote more than half in jest, this poet, friend of scientists and mathematicians (including Einstein), who twice renounced the practice of poetry for silence, appeals to reason on more than Platonist grounds It is not merely the condensation and obliqueness of poetry, placing such strains upon language as to remove the voice of the poem altogether from the realm of the vernacular it exploits. Tactics such as those of Berryman in the *Dream Songs* result in a special dialect analogous to those literary dialects reserved in classical languages for lyric, drama, or epic. Except perhaps for the famous Burma Shave verses of the thirties, language that functions as poetry is calculated to retard or obstruct the ordinary process of assimilation that is the norm for other modes of verbal communication. A small, specially trained audience to savor the difficulties has been the destiny of printed poetry.

Reading pure literature for enjoyment, so preeminent a part of nineteenth century life, has become a very marginal indulgence by the latter part of the twentieth century even for intellectuals judging by publishing trends. Naturally, to say that hardly anyone is reading them is not to deny the existence of serious writers, but merely to call attention to the expanding isolation of the writer of pure literature for whom even the universities have become ambiguous sponsors.

An age of Criticism has done less for literature than it has for a burgeoning bureaucracy whose existence is justified by the production of professional interpretations - - and bibliographies of the same. The New Criticism, salvific as it appeared to those who fervently embraced its protocols in the fifties, has proved almost as sterile as the unimaginative historicism it was meant to supplant because it has become institutionalized. It is not literature that has failed us, but we who have failed literature by making inappropriate demands upon it through a naive opportunism in the interests of cultural absolutism, by turning it over to the Ph.D. factories and Creative Writing Mills. Let us admit that the universities in their inflated Humanities departments - - now in embarrassed solicitation of an ever more depleted supply of students - - have never been so much the handmaidens of culture as they have been the reducers of culture into manageable pedagogical proportions. The melancholy, but in all probability axiomatic, likelihood is that to the extent that we profess "scientific" rigor as scholars our premises are undermined by the most transparent subjective impressionism of any intellectual discipline. The essays collected here, meditations on works upon which I have placed personal valuations, are not immune to this occupational disease. Moreover, they are based, as are the undergraduate themes one assigns, upon a language in the process of obsolescence, outverballed hourly in the electronic age outside our study doors.

Cultures differ enormously in the emphasis with which they respond to the invitation of the senses, and, further, in the manner in which they adapt their conceptual apparatus to the various senses. Walter Ong addresses this topic in his book, *The Presence of the Word*. In his own words:

Man's sensory perceptions are abundant and overwhelming. He cannot attend to them all at once.

> In great part a given culture teaches him one or another way of productive specialization. It brings him to organize his sensorium by attending to some types of perception more than others by making an issue of certain ones while relatively neglecting other ones. The sensorium is a fascinating focus for cultural studies. Given sufficient knowledge of the sensorium exploited within a specific culture, one could probably define the culture as a whole in virtually all its aspects.[4]

The sensorium of our age has changed before our eyes and the universities, or more particularly the English departments thereof, are unprepared to deal with the difference because it challenges their perception of their own identity as cultural absolutists. All our pieties toward the Judeo-Christian tradition have brought us, vacillating and equivocating, to the limbo of bankrupt individualism. So long as we in the western democracies are capable of purveying the unexamined premises of our latent self-detestation, narcissism will continue to be its own reward.

"But Capitalism works!" exclaimed one of my more intelligent colleagues one day. What works best of all upon the middle-aged academic in an age of anxiety is a familiar vocabulary sacramentalizing greed.

If the world survives the cataclysms incidental to this perspective, perhaps another generation will find its way beyond the confines of self-serving egoism to create a new literature celebrating a new kind of community.

FOOTNOTES

I THE DISAPPEARANCE OF LITERATURE

1. Paul Valéry, *Aesthetics,* translated by Ralph Mannheim (New York, 1964), p. 225.

2. Arnold Hauser, *The Social History of Art,* Vol. IV (London, 1962), p. 228.

3. Paul Valéry, *Occasions,* The Collected Works, Vol. II (Princeton, 1970), pp. 151-157.

4. W.J. Ong, *The Presence of the Word,* (New Haven, 1967), p. 6.

Chapter Two

RANDALL JARRELL AND THE ART OF SELF-DEFENSE

"A good poet", said Randall Jarrell, "is someone who manages, in a lifetime of standing out in thunderstorms, to be struck by lightning five or six times." I have a less attractive notion that poetry, like other highly determined forms of human behaviour, is part of that process of necessary rationalisation by which we maintain and render tolerable our imperfect lives. In our poems we convince ourselves, and sometimes others, that we are wiser, more perceptive, more innocent, more humane, more inspired, and more agreeable than is ever likely to have been the case.

If art as a form of self-construction holds certain perils as a mode of self-deception, they are perhaps nothing compared to the peril of seeing ourselves as we in fact are. Our humanity obliges us all to become deceivers in the interest of self-preservation. The poem is the poet's way of revising life, and as such it is by no means a dishonourable expression of self-defense.

In contradicting the naive biographical suppositions of Sainte-Beuve (into which the most backward student is unlikely to fall these days), Proust said: "Cette méthode méconnait ce qu'une fréquentation un peu profonde avec nous-mêmes nous apprend: qu'un livre est le produit d'un autre moi que celui que nous manifestons dans nos habitudes, dans la société, dans nos vices. Ce moi-là, si nous voulons essayer de la comprendre, c'est au fond de nous-mêmes, en essayant de la récréer en nous, que nous pouvons y parvenir. Rien ne peut nous dispenser de cet effort de notre coeur." (CONTRE SAINTE-BEUVE, Gallimard, p. 157.)

The desire for "sincerity" in art probably represents

a hopeless misconception of the kind of activity art is. On the other hand, doubtless the repute of sincerity as a criterion of anything suffers among us when we come to apprehend its tendency to be the professional characteristic most commonly encountered in swindlers, con men, imposters, and in those who wish to sell us something.

Jarrell's poems do not, I think, strike one as the work of a man who ever wasted much time standing around in the rain. There is more yankee ingenuity at his disposal than he might have wished to admit to. He is the sort who would have devised a method of simulating thunder and lightning while remaining quite dry himself. His poems indeed are remarkably rational in structure. No obscurity muddies, no ambiguity enriches, no imaginal density alters the straightforward, colloquial prose texture of his verse. Rather, it is his criticism that is given over to enthusiasm, to "surprise", to inspiration, to ecstatic lists. But Jarrell has something to sell and it seems to be his innocence. He would not be offended if we said of him, as he does in praise of Whitman, "How American". Yet I presume that this quality of the poems causes the greatest exasperation to many readers. For this ingenuousness can accompany the most abrasive, iron-clad complacence to be found anywhere outside the less attractive verse of Frost. "In Galleries", for example, surely does not have the desired effect of showing how the poet's simple heart is warmed by having the Virgin's tear pointed out to him by the shabby museum guard "in a fountain of Italian". It is altogether too insistent about the quaintness of poverty in foreign places and the mickey mouse money in which the tip is bestowed.

> But in Italy, sometimes, a guard is different.
> He is poorer than a guard would be at home - -
> How cheap his old uniform is, how dirty!
> . . . He speaks and smiles;
> And whether or not you understand Italian,

You understand he is human, and still hopes - -
And, smiling, repeating his *Bellissima!*
You give him a dime's worth of aluminum.

A more expressive effort on the guard's part earns him, at the end of the poem, "A quarter's worth of nickel and aluminum."

Jarrell's poems very effectively resist being thought about. What one is invariably tempted to think about instead is the unacknowledged Jarrell behind the poems, the shrewd and occasionally shrewish intelligence that sometimes filters through the good grey poet's beard in adult syntax in a child's voice: the Jarrell that no one will ever have known - - not his wife, his children, his cat Elfie, his newspaper boy Nestus Gurley, his colleagues, his students, his friends, least of all perhaps Randall Jarrell himself. That is the tragedy of the poems. The tragedy that never gets into the poems, whose surrogate is desperate make-believe - - when it is not mere gossip. For this is not the Greenwood, and he who wrote:

O arms that arm, for a child's wars, the child!

must have discovered how little assistance such weapons can be to grown-ups.

Yet how persistently these poems turn toward childhood, either for their subject matter or for a point of view - - as if the other self of the author, this cipher, could secure its ultimate fulfillment only by means of such radical substitutions. There is nothing new in this pattern of course - - nothing newer than the late eighteenth century at least - - and certainly something expressly familiar in American life: a middle class cultural dogma that preaches happiness and childhood as coterminous. Indeed, it is this conception of happiness as the fixed obligation of childhood that renders particularly difficult (and rare) the American male's arrival at adulthood at all. The weighty and unfulfillable requirements not merely to be happy one hundred percent of the time, but manifestly happier than mommy and daddy ever were, enslaves not a few in the Land of the Brave.

The island that the children ran is gone.
The island sang to me: *Believe! Believe!*
And didn't I know a lady with a lion?
Each evening as the sun sank, didn't I grieve
To leave *my* tree house for reality?
There was nothing there for me to disbelieve.
At peace among my weapons, I sit in my tree
And feel: *Friday night, then Saturday, then Sunday!*

. . . Liking that world where
The children eat, and grow giant and good,
I swear as I've often sworn: "I'll never forget
What it's like, when *I've* grown up."
. . . My lifetime
Got rid of, I sit in a dark blue sedan
Beside my great-grandmother, in Hollywood.
We pass a windmill, a pink sphinx, an Allbran
Billboard; thinking of Salammbo, Robin Hood,
The old prospector with his flapjack in the air,
I sit with my hands folded: I am good.

Whether one finds this more wonderful than pathetic or more pathetic than fatuous depends upon the proportions of one's enthusiasm (or lack of enthusiasm) for Wordsworth, Charles Dodgson, J.M. Barrie - - or Freud. If there is another ghost hovering over this enterprise, it is not from the poet's favorite country; it is the plump Gallic shadow of J.J. Rousseau.

One of the curiosities of the Lost World of Jarrell, depicted with such unabating nostalgia in the later poems, is the complete isolation of the idealized child. Not a single human playmate intervenes to modify either the child's communion with himself or his idyllic relations with the unfailingly benevolent adults with whom his life is implicated. ("At last I go to Mama in her gray/silk, to Pop, to Dandeen in her black/ silk. I put my arms around them, they/Put their arms around me. Then I go back/To my bedroom; I read as I undress/ . . . Mama calls 'Is your light out?' I call back, 'Yes', /And turn the light out.") The burden of sentiment that accompanies these revelations of good behaviour simply emphasizes the fantasied nature of the material. Whatever interest such an event has is unlikely to be literary. Blakean innocence, in contrast, is always reflected in useful collaboration with experience. The constriction and impoverishment of consciousness that occur in regression are evident in Jarrell's early work and pervasive and uncontrolled in the later poems: the tissue of wishes that stands for transliterated autobiography. Thus the poet whom we should most like to believe is not the most convincing presence in these poems.

Unlike most lyric poems which begin in language, Jarrell's consistently originate in fabulation, in make-believe. He was at pains always to construct his verse out of language that "cats and dogs can understand". Metrical values are frequently subordinated to this interest, or only perfunctiorily observed.

Mnemonic rituals of repetition, suggesting the incantations associated with children's games, are his most conspicuous trick of style:

> These were wishes. The glass in which I saw
> Somewhere else, someone else: the field upon which
> sprawled
> Dead, and the ruler of the dead, my twin - -
> Were wishes? Hansel, by the eternal sea,
> Said to the flounder for this first wish, *Let me wish*
> *And let my wish be granted;* it was granted.
> Granted, granted . . .
>
> ("The Marchen")

One of the unresolved problems of Jarrell's work, and its only notable source of tension, is the way in which his wit conflicts with his pathos. Those poems in which wit, even if unkindly, wins at the expense of the warm, cuddly, wondering, wish-fulfilling infantilism are to my mind the only poems that wear at all well. "A Girl In A Library", about a student of Home Economics and Physical Education falling asleep over books too difficult for her, succeeds admirably. The effaced narrator clearly expresses his superiority to his subject in an imaginary conversation with Tatiana Larina who is looking out at the scene from a copy of Pushkin's "Eugen Onegin".

But my mind, gone out in tenderness,
Shrinks from its object with a thoughtful sigh.
This is a waist the spirit breaks its arm on.
The gods themselves, against you, struggle in vain.
This broad, low strong-boned brow; these heavy eyes;
These calves, grown muscular with certainties;
This nose, three medium-sized pink strawberries
- - But I exaggerate. In a little you will leave:
I'll hear, half-squeal, half shriek, your laugh of greeting -
Then *decrescendo,* bars of that strange speech
In which each sound sets out to seek each other,
Murders its own father, marries its own mother,
And ends as one grand transcendental vowel.
(Yet for all I know, the Egyptian Helen spoke so.)
As I look, the world contracts around you:
I see Brunnhilde had brown braids and glasses
She used for studying; Salome straight brown bangs. . .
The trap has closed about you and you sleep.
If someone questioned you, *What doest thou here?*
You'd knit your brows like an orangoutang
(But not so sadly; not so thoughtfully)
And answer with a pure heart, guilelessly:
I'm studying . . .
                    If only you were not!

The poet's distance as observer - - patronizing or not - - keeps the treacliness out.

Reading these poems, one almost wishes that Robert

Frost had never existed. But if he had not existed, Randall Jarrell would surely have invented him - - only to improve upon the old man in his own way. Jarrell's sensitive reading of Frost, reprinted in his collection of essays, *Poetry And The Age,* reveals a canny ear for the defects as well as the effects of the writer whose influence upon his works is perhaps greater than any other. Yet, having discerned the flaws of greatness, he reproduced them as well rather faithfully in his uneven poems. The public posture of the sentimental determinist is maintained with unequal conviction. Jarrell's progress as a poet cannot, I think, be measured by stages of technical experiment. His approach to the poem never appreciably changed. It is his mimetic instinct for pretending his way into other peoples' lives, of trying on identities that matters. The role of the poet as "liar" really attracted him most. This is the basis of his appreciation of Whitman, whom he praises in "Poetry And The Age" for "having wonderful dreams, telling wonderful lies", and it forms the argument of a very amusing poem called "A Conversation with the Devil", in which the devil reports:

> I once saw a tenor at the Opera Comique
> Who played the Fisher - - of Pearls or else of Souls.
> He wore a leopard-skin, lay down and died;
> And sang ten minutes lying on his side
> And died again; and then, applauded,
> Gave six bows, leaning on his elbow,
> And at the seventh started on his encore.
> He was, I think, a poet.

But Jarrell specializes in what he would call "the dailiness of life" of which his penchant for fairy tales is a well-integrated part. His range includes a crotchety old moneybags, a well-todo invalid, a boy dreaming of a journey to the North Pole, a middle aged woman at the super market, a sick child, children deprived of their mothers by war or chance, soldiers and citizens of every age and status. The war poems have been widely liked, but they seem to me on the whole as romantically and imperfectly imagined as a dated and familiar host of B movies. So I pass over these war poems without comment, for they have never lacked able defenders, to the spinsters who exercised such an attraction over Jarrell and who are among his most authentic representations.

Possibly his best sustained performance in this genre is to be found in "The End of the Rainbow", a long poem about a maiden lady, an amateur painter of land and seascapes, transplanted from her native New England scene ("of Ipswich,/ A sampler cast upon a savage shore") to sunny southern California with her little Pekinese dog, one of a series all named Su-Su. She is delineated with the touch of Ransom as having: "The hands of a lady left out in the weather / Of resorts; the face of a fine girl left out in the years." Her dreaming, self-absorbed retreat from Life is picked out in the insignificance of its details - - the date milkshake and avocadoburger she has for lunch, her bedtime reading from "Compensation" (". . . or else the Scriptures / With a *Key* by Mrs. Eddy"), thoughts of the Frog-Prince (transformed at one point from a friendly suitor to a formidable father) - - with the attentive application of a fellow-fantasist.

Beside her, Death
Or else Life - - spare, white, permanent - -
Works out their *pas de dux*: here's Death
Arranging a still life for his own Content;
Death walking Su-Su; Death presenting
To the trustees of the estate, a varid
Portfolio; Death digging
For gold at the end of the rainbow - - strikes water,
Which is thinner than blood; strikes oil,
That water will not mix with - - no, nor blood;
Pauses, mops his skull, says: *The wrong end.*

After children, well-heeled eccentrics hold a distinguished place in his pantheon of subjects. ("The secret that the grownups share", he observed in "The Lost World", "is what to do to make money.") But of course his governing interest, his artist's curiosity were primarily addressed to the question: what to do to make life. If memory, if nostalgia for an irrecoverable innocence often threatened to falsify or proved a soggy trap for this poet, the alien, mysterious, imaginable secrets of other persons' personalities provided a happy release. Now that death - - or life - - has taken him back, who would have the heart to blame him for affinities to Peter Pan rather than to Proust?

Chapter Three

PAUL VALÉRY: THE ART OF CONCEALMENT

Fifty years after the publication of *Le Cimetière Marin* and twenty-five years after the death of its author, we continue to meditate his example without fear of exhausting it. Yet the example is surely one of the most enigmatic in modern letters, for Valéry puzzles us at his most lucid and, where other writers would be conspicuous in their works, takes us unaware by his quite practiced absence. Indeed, a persistent attraction of this writer lies in the curiously tentative and provisional relation of his mind to the texts in which it was his desire to represent the procedures of his own consciousness.

A willing prisoner of polite society and public life, Paul Valéry may well be unique in convincing posterity of his singular literary genius without actually having produced the canon of masterworks of which he was clearly capable. He rather insisted upon the incidental nature of his writings, upon the fact that everything he allowed to be published had been commissioned (for the most part for rhetorical public occasions), even preferring to designate his poems as "exercises" whose interest for him lay almost exclusively in the process of their composition rather than the finished product. This withholding of commitment to a final form of the sort common to the serious artist amounts to commitment of another and particularly intriguing kind. And this studied public presence under whose auspices a program of rigorously sustained self-examination is conducted, represents narcissism with a difference. For, if, under the aegis of analysis, Valéry composed several of the finest poems in the language, they were poems conceived not only as "manoeuvres" but also as efforts having no other aim than the reconstruction of self.

On wonders nonetheless whether Valéry's resumption of the practice of poetry differs in character from his twenty-year abstention. The art of poetry as he practiced it implies a profound, even an expressly clinical, disengagement from the self, even while an hypothesized self, a mental construct is its overt end. That for Valéry the act of writing consisted in the renunciation of a buried self seems to me equally plausible. Distrust of language, distrust of the world may be construed as ancillary expressions of a primary mistrust of self, and this writer whose acknowledged reservations attest to a continuing preoccupation, who again and again felt prompted to speculate upon the topic of suicide, may have found in the poems, as it seems he had anticipated in pure thought, an effective alternative to self-annihilation.

* * *

Allowing form to discover content is a procedure habitual to the lyric poet, but the man who recognized in himself *"l'ame opposable"* would not favor leaving it to its own uncontained devices. Although he celebrated the *"Douceur d'être et de n'être pas" ("Les Pas", Charmes)*, and though absence remained one of his favorite words, his manner of using it suggests that he endows this term with metaphysical implications associated with his efforts toward self-knowledge. The notebooks and prose are full of references to the examined consciousness. That region of the mind he had, in his own words, "abandoned and even fled from" can only have been the unconscious.

Coinciding as his career does with the decline of symbolism and the ascendant surrealist wave of dreams, Valéry has been taken as an example of a great mind whose historical circumstances precluded his achieving the artistic fulfillment his gifts warranted. His world was intellectually a nineteenth century world. No one appreciated the subversiveness of the life of the mind more than Valéry (except perhaps Stendhal).

He is revolutionary, not negatively through acts of refusal, but through his acts of acceptance carried to unforeseen extremes. He accepts the established cultural order, but only on his own terms, those of a most dangerous diplomatist adhering to the rules of a game. One is left asking oneself in this mirror world of ostensible order: but what *is* the game? And what is the pretext for the game? Gazing off obliquely into space from the photographed cover of the Pleiade edition of his *Oeuvres*, for all the world like a department store dummy or an Italian barber, the author is no help.

So masculine and clear a mind was bound to recoil from the dubious indulgences of dadaism. While the surrealists dreamed wishfully of being dominated by their poems, Valéry expressed his scepticism of inspiration in no uncertain terms, stating that he should infinitely prefer to achieve a feeble work in complete consciousness rather than the most beautiful piece in a trance. This will to dominate the poem rather than to be dominated by it becomes the unspoken premise of every utterance. *"A la moindre rature,"* he says, *"le principe d'inspiration totale est ruiné. - - L'intelligence efface ce que le dieu a imprudemment crée."*

Of course the most infallible way of dominating the work of art is not to make it at all, and the curious preponderance in Valéry's writings of elegant journalism and exhaustive notebooks, of dialogues in which art is talked about over poems in which art is achieved, suggests that he resorted to this method consistently over the years. "In literature," he said, "the true is not conceivable", reminding us of Wallace Stevens whose "fiction" was his word for "truth". In another and absolutely provisional sense, the truth for Valéry may be equated quite simply with work, the puritan answer to anxiety. One detects a prophetic irony in the infant Valéry's first recorded word: *"clef"*. Keys are for locking things up as well as for unlocking. And we are never unaware in reading Valéry (or his mentor Mallarmé) that consciousness in such a writer is collaborating in a work of concealment far in excess of what we presume the occasion to have been. "La Jeune Parque" is five hundred lines long, a mystifying poem whose readers have not even yet come to general agreement as to its subject. The product of countless deletions over the more than four years devoted to its composition, suppressed portions of this poem are said to amount to more than a page in manuscript for each line retained.

Valéry made a classic recommendation in his little book, *Degas, Danse, Dessin,* that he has himself followed with scrupulous exactitude:

> *Achever un ouvrage consiste a faire disparaitre tout ce qui montre ou suggère sa fabrication. L'artiste ne doit, selon cette condition surannée, s'accuser que par son style, et doit soutenir son effort jusqu'a ce que le travail ait éfface les traces du travail.*

Work effaces work in the poems of the master, but it also effaces more than work. Perhaps it is not too much to say that work under this rubric is ordained to the demolition of conceptual form. The disappearing acts performed by Mallarmé and Valéry both incorporate and go beyond Flaubert's stipulation that the artist ought to be in his work like God in his creation, invisible and all-powerful, that he should be felt everywhere but remain unseen. Flaubert, too, expressed a much-misunderstood wish to write a work "about nothing". And Valéry, who remarked in *Tel Quel* that "poetry is nothing but literature reduced to the essential of its active principle" added that "the subject of a poem is as strange and also as important to the author as his own name is." Yet he distinguishes in due course two sorts of verse: "les vers donnés et les vers calculés."

> Les vers calculés sont ceux qui se presentent necessairement sous forme de problèmes à resoudre - et qui ont pour conditions initiales d'abord les vers donnés, et ensuite la rime, la syntaxe, le sens déjà engagé par ses données. . .

To be always on the side of calculation, as Valéry was, is to require the intervention of form in a substantive role; form in Valéry *is* the subject as well as the active principle. Henri Focillon in his *Vie des Formes* affirms that the power of the formal order alone authorises the competency of creation, its spontaneous character, whereas the state of indeterminate liberty conduces fatally to imitation. The immense variety of techniques required in the genealogy of a work of art attests that the principle of all technique is not inertia but action. (pp. 24-25)

Poems as different from Valéry's as the Cantos of Pound have baffled readers for similar reasons: although their ingredients were readily identifiable, their subjects proved elusive. The Cantos have been aptly described as "a voice without a subject". Valéry appreciated (as all artists instinctively must) that poetry is not a proper medium for thought, but that to construct a poem containing nothing but poetry is equally impossible. A poem embodies what T.S. Eliot termed "felt thought", as *experience*, with all the implications in the human scheme of a complex rapport in the reciprocal relations of emotion with intelligence. "La Jeune Parque" confounds our philosophical expectations by enacting the very movements of consciousness. Music and not ratiocination is its analogue. He called this poem "a revery of which the waking consciousness is at the same time neither subject nor object." The intellectual content of the poem is not reducible to *meaning* this or that, but instead is transformed into a dynamic principle. The play of the mind becomes literally the main actor in a drama of consciousness. And the experience of thought is enacted along with its characteristic hesitations, hiatuses, disjunctions, elisions and false starts. The drama is in the drama rather than any denouement; in the problems to be solved rather than their resolution.

If a poem has a voice, does it, after all, require more?

A voice has its own momentum, creates its own trajectory and implies auditors. We should ask rather what the voice accomplishes in given instances, to what areas of consciousness it lends expression. But surely to require of the poet only those forms of organization congenial to the prose mind reflects a misunderstanding of the nature of poetry. A poem is a linear arrangement. Yet the "sense" of a poem, however anchored in its syntax, is rarely if ever reducible to the consecutiveness of its elements. The radical departures in the poems of Valéry are, as a matter of fact, precisely disguised by their conventional surfaces.

Certain poems which fail or only partially succeed leave us with the impression that the poet has been fighting the wrong war, misapprehending his enemies for his friends, and being vulnerable in ways he does not himself understand. Books, in Valéry's estimation, have the same enemies as man, not least among these being their own contents. He said that either thoughts or emotions entirely naked (as they tend to be in the works of the immature artist) are as defenseless as naked men. So far as the artist is concerned, the most effective way of "clothing" them is by supplying their proper *rapports*. Form, even when represented simply by a voice, becomes thus not a substitute for reality but a contribution to it.

The self-understanding of even the greatest artists is bound, by reason of the very humanity that provides its grounds, to be limited and imperfect. And indeed those passages in our literature that impress us as most luminous revelations of the human predicament proceed often enough from precisely those dark areas of his mental experience that are least accessible to the writer's rational understanding. Moreover, the book or poem that an author writes may very well happen not to be the book or poem he thought he was writing. Under the criterion of consciousness, Valéry came upon an intuition that defines his own dualistic growth as a poet. He may have been the last person to comprehend the implications of the insight even though he wrestled for a whole lifetime with its consequences in his mental life. In *Tel Quel* he notes: *La pensee a les deux sexes: se feconde et se porte soi-même."*

The human psyche in its most primitive state is, according to Jung, androgynous. The animus and the anima carry on a perpetual dialogue in us all and are in varying degrees dominant or recessive in a poet's work. Gaston Bachelard in his remarkable book, *The Poetics of Reverie*, says that reverie (governed by the feminine principle) can help us know language without censorship. And he defends the thesis that *"reverie is under the sign of the anima.* When reverie is truly profound, the being who comes to dream with us is our *"anima"*. (p. 62) This, surely, is the *"Harmonieuse moi"* at the heart of "La Jeune Parque", whereas the *animus* presides with consummate authority over "Le Cimetiere Marin":

> Beau ciel, vrai ciel, regarde-moi qui change!
> Après tant d'orgueil, après tant d'étrange
> Oisiveté, mais pleine de pouvoir,
> Je m'abandonne à ce brillant espace,
> Sur les maisons des morts mon ombre passe
> Qui m'apprivoise à son frele mouvoir.

It would be an impertinence for the critic to assume the role of amateur psychologist and pretend to diagnose the changing relations of *animus* to *anima* in Valéry's obsessively self-observing mental history. We have the notebooks, the dialogues, the speeches - - program notes for the concert of a strangely publicised interior life - - and a few poems, among the most impressive but also most devalued of his productions.

This devaluation of poetry as an enterprise is one of the anomalies of Valéry's career. Was he merely disingenuous, merely exercising a sophisticated form of self-protection? What purpose otherwise is served by the insistence that he undertook no self-initiated creative tasks outside the notebooks? His approach to poetry as a series of problems to be solved is of course highly professional. And so is his notion of the poet's duty to language:

> Le poète se consacre et se consume donc à definir et à construire un langage dans le langage; et son operation, qui est longue, difficile, delicate, qui demande les qualités les plus diverses de l'esprit, et qui jamais n'est achevée comme jamais elle n'est exactement possible, tend à constituer le discours d'un etre plus pur, plus puissant et plus profond dans ses pensées, plus intense dans sa vie, plus élégant et plus heureux dans sa parole que n'importe quelle personne réelle. Cette parole extraordinaire se fait connaitre et reconnaitre par le rythme et les harmonies qui la soutiennent et qui doivent être si intimement, et même mysterieuse liés a sa generation, que le son et le sens ne se puissent plus séparer et se repondent indéfiniment dans la memoire.

("Situation de Baudelaire," *Oeuvres*, p. 611)

Potentially great and developing poets are usually recognizable by their capacity for using up and transcending their influences. Strange to say, Valéry never divested himself of his most compelling influences, and they are a decidedly limited lot: Huysmans, Edgar Poe (that perpetual snare and delusion to the French literary imagination), Pierre Louys, Mallarmé. He began his career by soliciting the approval of Mallarmé and resumed it after long abstention with an imitation of the "Herodiade". Yet the truth of the matter may be something other. In a very real sense, and despite the rhetorical correspondence in his work to superficial literary conventions, Valéry is perhaps not strictly a "literary" writer at all, even though he remains a writer's writer *par excellence.*

His real dependence was never upon exclusively literary precedents but centered upon those aspects of the meditated world which provided him the necessary clues for entering into the mystery of his origin and discovering the deepest potential of his renewed self-hood. Sea, sky, space, sun are more than mirrors, more than metaphors, the outer signs of chaos circumnavigated, sensuous extensions of the concealed life of the mind.

Chapter Four

HART CRANE'S UNIMPROVED INFANCY

The extraordinary openness of Hart Crane's personality given the emotive conditions of his existence, must have contributed as much as anything to his ruin. In his openness Crane differs markedly from the usual homosexual pattern, for the society that has commonly required homosexuals to be covert in their dealings with one another seems to conduce to fairly elaborate social defenses. Yet one does not have to read very far in Crane's biography or the published correspondence (which is as lucid as the poems are opaque) to conclude that he was a person utterly lacking in defenses. His demands upon friendship were gargantuan but manifestly without guile. He was not a manipulator of persons. If he regularly evoked unexampled generosity from his acquaintances, it is undoubtedly because his demands were so clearly and urgently the demands of a child. And so, I think, were his demands upon literature.

One thinks of a life pursued with such unabating and gregarious enthusiasm as Crane's as expressing the will to live and, above all, the power to survive. There is little evidence in the meticulously documented accounts that Crane was - - as most poets require to be - - reclusive or withdrawn. People and alcohol in large quantities were his staple. From the dreary, violent and prolonged attrition of his parents' disastrous relationship he fled, not to solitude, but to multiply loyalties of his own. His enthusiasm, one comes to discern, is the very element of his despair. The abundant energies, the remarkable stamina, the sheer appetitive drive of his curiosity should all have put him permanently on the side of life. His biographers agree however that quite early on even these qualities were turned to pathetically destructive uses. A photograph in Unterecker's book, *Voyager, A Life of Hart Crane,* taken a few months before the move to New York prompted by the intention of preparing for the university entrance that never took place, shows the young poet looking at least twice his seventeen years . . . more years in fact than he was ever to attain.

Crane's resources were not of the wrong sort for surviving - - even the entanglements of so thoroughly frightening a woman as his mother. They were resources simply and consistently misapplied. (How could a poet ever have supposed, at least after trial and error, that writing advertising copy for Sweet's catalogue would interfere less with his exalted vocation than tossing boxes in his daddy's candy factory, hewing and hauling, or shipping out as a sailor? Despite his demonic energies, Crane maintained a fastidious distance from anything resembling manual labor to the end of his life.) Literature has not, for the great writers, been merely a distraction from their problems. Rather it has been a means of meeting and transforming those least bearable of psychic burdens into a masterable order. Crane was unable, or fundamentally unwilling, to convert this most troubled area of his life into art. He seems to have sought intoxication with the desperate aim of finding poetry when he was outside himself in some impossibly other state of consciousness. The unconscious is not so easily dispensed with, but Crane in his poems, most notably in "The Bridge", persistently attempted affirmations that contradicted his own deepest experience. And he protected this program with some curiously inflated rhetoric upon occasion, remarkable for its failure to correspond to his actual practice when writing poems. Said he, "For poetry is an architectural art, based not on Evolution or the idea of progress, but on the articulation of the contemporary human consciousness *sub specie aeternitatis,* and inclusive of all readjustments incident to science and other shifting factors related to that consciousness," And later in the same essay: "For unless poetry can absorb the machine, i.e., *acclimatize* it as naturally and casually as trees, cattle, galleons, castles and all other human associations of the *past*, then poetry has failed of its full contemporary function." 1

In actual practice, Crane employed poetry, it seems to me, in the simplest romantic mode: to escape an indelible psychic reality, to embrace a fantasmal alternative, an abstract ideal of "absolute beauty". For, whatever else he was writing about, he wrote always about being a poet. So did Keats, so did Shelley who also died young and whose poems, like Crane's tend to be more interesting for the kinds of mistakes they incorporate, for the unfulfilled possibilities they exhibit, than for the perfection of accomplished art. It happens that these three Romantics resemble each other as well in being in large part self-educated, which meant in effect largely uneducated. (Some would dispute this point which to me nevertheless remains self-evident. Indeed, to my mind the Romantics exemplify the fact that natural intelligence is not incompatible with large areas of ignorance. Coleridge is the exception.)

Great and good poets may frequently write "better than they know", but not in ignorance. Unfortunately for the Romantics poetry becomes at its worst a diligent flirtation with ignorance, and at its best a sometimes desperate form of exhibitionism. The death-wishing Romantic, in displaying not what he feels and knows but what he wills, is led into characteristic falsifications. "The correspondent breeze" and the language of bombast are rather intimately related commodities in literary history. (Crane's substitution of "corymbulous formations of mechanics" for airplanes in Part III of "For the Marriage of Faustus and Helen"is not different in kind, though less economical, than the eighteenth century's "finny tribe" for fishes.) Keats himself was astute enough to notice how much more often the Romantics managed to produce impressive lines than successful poems.

These remarks are not made to disparage Crane's authentic and superior gifts - - he was at least Keats' equal - -

but to suggest how such gifts failed to issue in more nearly perfect poems. It is because he refused or only inadvertently accepted the subjects that crowded upon him from within while expending his resources in a vain pursuit of the chimerical abstraction that he permitted himself as subject. No poet ever took his apprenticeship more seriously. It was the one way whereby the embattled child could rescue himself from the indignity of the marital contentions in which he found himself a pawn. But neither, one supposes, has the muse ever been propitiated by more strenuous and self-defeating means. The dionysian frenzies produced by bootleg liquor and jazz music that were Crane's approach to composition had self-evident limitations. Indeed they are less obviously means of expanding consciousness than of obliterating it. Aside from being patently "romantic" choices, they appear to be choices inspired by ambivalent motives, motives of the sort that countenance suicide by rehearsing it. When friends saw the tree outside Crane's window festooned with typewriter ribbon, they knew that he had been composing. They might have guessed as well that an infant had awakened from his dream of omnipotence to cry for help. At the memorable Fourth of July celebration that resulted in two poems, "Passage" and "Wine Menagerie", a sober guest reports having observed Crane sitting by the lilacs in the dooryard at Slater Brown's meditatively pouring a box of salt upon the turning phonograph and repeating to himself: Where the cedar leaf divides the sky . . . where the cedar leaf divides the sky . . . I was promised an improved infancy." According to the ironies of life and art, such promises are fulfillable only provisionally in dreams, or poems. But the dreams that are fruitful for poetry are criticisms of reality, not substitutions for it.

It is not in being morbid that Crane falters as a poet, but in not being morbid enough. A compulsive and priggish optimism mars the myth-making of "The Bridge". The bridge that needed building was a different one altogether, to which Walt

Whitman would have had nothing to contribute.

Requiring literature to be better than life, and confident that he had it in him to become the "Pindar of the machine age" - - without perceiving, as Pound had, what a windbag his examplar was - - Crane set about planning the lone poem in which he aimed to capture "the myth of America". Few poems have been accorded the friendly attention "The Bridge" received, from its planning and painful execution to its final mixed reception: Crane's background reading, Crane's sponsorship by Otto Kahn, Crane's room overlooking the object of his symbolic imaginings, the Brooklyn Bridge (the same room formerly occupied by Roebling, the bridge's architect), Crane's visions and revisions, his travels, the preludes to ever more spectacular binges, augmented by his belated estrangement and panic-stricken flight from his mother. During the years between February 1923 and the winter of 1930 while the poem, conceived in transcendental terms as an act of acceptance and assimilation, was going forward by fits and starts, the poet's life was getting more and more out of hand. The sanctity of impulse, the surrender to instinct, the abnegation of reason that confounded the poem in its conceptual form proved lethal off the printed page. The greater the gifts brought to such assumptions, the more impressive the wreckage that results.

Because Crane responded to language intuitively rather than ratiocinatively ("the bridge is becoming a ship, a world, a woman, a tremendous harp . . .", Crane wrote to Waldo Frank) his poem is really a succession of beginnings, in varying degrees brilliant and banal, and probably would always have been so, even if he had had greater control over his life at the time of writing. Along with a number of magnificent images ("Down Wall, from girder into street noon leaks, / A rip-tooth of the sky's acetylene . . .") remain some of the least felicitous lines in the language. But had Crane ever got round to attending Columbia University as he had intended, chances are that - - being a bright lad - - he would have learned enough not to risk his newly gained command of words on a topic so sophomoric, so contrary to his own experience and so untrue to history.

Out of the personal turmoil of this period came some humanly restorative gains. Best of all was the discovery after many years of hostility and suspicion that his father, now about to be happily re-married and residing in Chagrin Falls, Ohio, was not the philistine monster he had been made out to be by Hart's mother. He had in fact been the generous supplier of cheques that bailed Hart regularly out of debt.

The point that needs to be appreciated and that is represented in exhaustive detail in Unterecker's book is the extent to which "The Bridge" was effectively a combined effort calling for the total commitment of literally dozens of individuals who fed and sheltered Crane (in one instance the hospitality had to consist in a shared tent and camp stove), who sobered him up, kept vigils at his bedside when he suffered from delirium tremens or provided him with fresh supplies of his favorite whiskey, Cutty Sark, who extricated him from difficulties with the law on two continents, and ultimately typed his chaotic manuscripts for him.

Crane labored, certainly, under strains it would be difficult to exaggerate. Yet from his youth to the end of his brief life he never lacked the kind of recognition that a writer most needs and all too seldom enjoys: that of his peers. The best poets of his, or any, generation gave him unstintingly of their time, their sympathy, their intelligent interest and creative criticism. They got his book published, prefaced and reviewed, and they wrote unsolicited letters of recommendation toward his Guggenheim award. It would be fatuous to contend that he or his art was cut down in the ideological crossfire of the twenties. Quite the contrary, he was doubtless kept alive longer by the non-partisan efforts of a few poets. Those who read his poems with reservations were among his most qualified readers. Biographical criticism is easily suspect and often irrelevant, but in the case of Hart Crane whose poems were so obviously written at the expense of the life, we can scarcely understand one while ignoring the other. Least of all can we ignore his literary parents, the Tates, the Browns, the Burkes who sympathized, sponsored and saw through his work.

Never were poems more clearly the product of unimproved infancy. Their omissions are likewise a product of that fact. Crane was unready in his immaturity to assimilate the best advice any poet could have received. Wanting to be a public poet when his material was intensely private was his greatest mistake. Towards the end, when he was living in Mexico and his alcoholic disintegration had reached epic proportions, his neighbour Katherine Anne Porter relates: ". . . he would talk slowly in an ordinary voice, saying he knew he was destroying himself as a poet, he did not know why, and he asked himself why, constantly. He said once that the life he lived was blunting his sensibilities, that he was no longer capable of feeling anything except under the most violent shocks: 'and I can't even then deceive myself that I really feel anything', he said. He talked about Baudelaire and Marlowe, and Whitman and Melville and Blake - - all the consoling examples he could call to mind of artists who had lived excessively in one way or another. Later, drunk, he would weep and shout, shaking his fist, 'I am Baudelaire, I am Whitman, I am Christopher Marlowe, I am Christ' but never once did I hear him say he was Hart Crane. . ." (quoted by Unterecker, p. 659).

Crane's best poems are among the earliest, published in *White Buildings,* and they persistently prefigure his death at sea. "At Melville's Tomb" and "Voyages" are freighted with recurrent water images that stand for sleep, death, desire and the summons of the creative unconscious.

AT MELVILLE'S TOMB

Often beneath the wave, wide from this ledge
The dice of drowned men's bones he saw bequeath
An embassy. Their numbers as he watched,
Beat on the dusty shore and were obscured.

And wrecks passed without sound of bells,
The calyx of death's bounty giving back
A scattered chapter, livid hieroglyph,
The portent wound in corridors of shells.

Then in the circuit calm of one vast coil,
Its lashings charmed and malice reconciled,
Frosted eyes there were that lifted altars;
And silent answers crept across the stars.

Compass, quadrant and sextant contrive
No farther tides . . . High in the azure steeps
Monody shall not wake the mariner.
This fabulous shadow only the sea keeps.

The perfection of this poem is that it means what it implies as well as what it "says". The implications are fully available to the attentive reader. The condensation is functional and therefore luminous in its specificity. All too often the density of Crane's lines is a sign that he is not coping with his material and the resulting poems do not succeed in being about their ostensible subjects. It is not wilful obscurantism that causes such clotting - - Crane worked painfully, conscientiously seriously, sometimes saving and re-using lines from discarded poems as new versions took shape - - but some sort of psychological log-jam of contending impressions within the mind. And of course the denotative aspect of words interested him far less than their associative powers. One senses then the poet's will forcing more acceptable aspirations toward meaning onto a poem. There are verses that say, again and again, I am poet, I am Faustus, or Christ, but not, I am Hart Crane.

The waste of Crane's creative genius is one of the tragedies of a devastatingly wasteful century. That waste, diligently itemized in Mr. Unterecker's book, will probably continue to have the fascination that natural disasters evoke, a focus for the guilty attentions of those who might in their libraries and classrooms have been less mesmerized by the poems that were never written. The bottom of the sea is cruel, but the unrealized expectations of one's self and the world are crueler.

For Crane, the invitation of the word was the invitation of death. His most prophetic poem, the sixth of the "Voyages", is virtually his only wholly serene one. Expression here does not compete with the inexpressible.

Where icy and bright dungeons lift
Of swimmers their lost morning eyes,
And ocean rivers, churning, shift
Green borders under stranger skies,

Steadily as a shell secretes
Its beating leagues of monotone,
Or as many waters through the sun's
Red kelson past the cape's wet stone;

O rivers mingling toward the sky
And harbor of the phoenix' breast - -
My eyes pressed black against the prow,
- - Thy derelict and blinded guest

Waiting afire, what name unspoke
I cannot claim: let they waves rear

More savage than the death of kings,
Some splintered garland for the seer.

Beyond siroccos harvesting
The solstice thunders, crept away,
Like a cliff swinging or a sail
Flung into April's inmost day - -

Creation's blithe and petalled word
To the lounged goddess when she rose
Conceding dialogue with eyes
That smile unsearchable repose - -

Still Fervid covenant, Belle Isle,
-- Unfolded floating dais before
Which rainbows twine continual hair - -
Belle Isle, white echo of the oar!

The imaged Word, it is, that holds
Hushed willows anchored in its glow.
It is the unbetrayable reply
Whose accent no farewell can know.

In this classically calm statement he seems to accept the identity assigned him by the sea, the extension of the unconscious, mirror and container of the problems and possibles of us all.

Chapter Three
FOOTNOTES

1. ("Modern Poetry", first published in a book by Oliver M. Sayler called *Revolt In The Arts: A Survey Of The Creation, Distribution And Appreciation Of Art In America*, New York, Brentano's, 1930.)

Chapter Five

JOHN BERRYMAN: THE WILL TO EXCEED

"The road of excess leads to the palace of wisdom."

(Blake)

At any given time anywhere one may be sure that very few memorable poems are being written by anyone. John Berryman's *77 Dream Songs* (1964), described as portions of a longer poem in progress, like his *Homage to Mistress Bradstreet* (1956) before it, constitute a major literary event: the genuine article in an era whose accredited masterpieces tend with predictable monotony to be feats of public relations rather than literary phenomena. As such, Berryman's poems are more clearly related, though not derivatively, to certain works that precede them - - to Hopkins for example in the 19th century or Wyatt in the 16th - - than to those of lesser contemporaries. In any case, it is always the minor poets who accommodate themselves to trends and are to be located in "movements" or "schools". To identify Berryman, then, with the "confessional" poets is to say nothing very useful about the poems, and to ignore the long-standing relation of all post-Wordsworthian poetry in English to itself. The writing of poems remains a solitary task. If poets have in common now above all an intensified self-consciousness, it is through the conditions of existence which they share rather than any literary code to which they have fallen heir.

Lacking the tyrannous comfort of an assured and identifiable public, the American writer has from the beginning been forced to invent his language and his audience anew with each successive work. This has led to extravagance and opaqueness in our most admired classics. It has ensured that even our dionysian poets have not written truly public poems but, like their apollonian counterparts, deeply schizoid and mannerist ones.

Berryman's gifts have never been at odds with his very considerable intelligence. Educated at Columbia University and Clare College, Cambridge, later teaching at Princeton, Harvard and Minnesota, author of a study of Stephen Crane, expositor of Thomas Nashe's 16th-century novel, *Jack the Unfortunate Traveller*, Berryman nevertheless as a poet in no way conforms to the restrictive limits of academic poetry. Moreover, from the outset of his carrer (his first book of poems, *The Dispossessed,* was published in 1948) there has been no evidence in his work of uncertainty regarding his function as a poet. His earliest published poems exhibit the maturity, the confidence, the range of imagination available only to artists of the first order. Yet the experience of being an American poet is the experience of being denied a *literary* function by a society that has never resolved - - even in its universities - - the ambivalent tensions between its profound distrust of the products of the mind an an undiscriminated will to "self-improvement". The perfect uselessness of art is a notion that, in America, only a minority of practicing artists is ever likely to entertain without discomfort.

Many of those who are now discovering the *Dream Songs* will not remember or recognize Berryman as the author of such a poem as his early "Winter Landscape":

The three men coming down the winter hill
In brown, with tall poles and a pack of hounds
At heel, through the arrangement of the trees
Past the five figures at the burning straw,
Returning cold and silent to their town,

Returning to the drifted snow, the rink
Lively with children, to the older men,
The long companions they can never reach,
The blue light, men with ladders, by the church
The sledge and shadow in the twilit street,

Are not aware that in the sandy time
To come, the evil waste of history
Outstretched, they will be seen upon the brow
Of that same hill: when all their company
Will have been irrecoverably lost,

These men, this particular three in brown
Witnessed by birds will keep the scene and say
By their configuration with the trees,
The small bridge, the red houses and the fire,
What place, what time, what morning occasion

Sent them into the wood, a pack of hounds
At heel and the tall poles upon their shoulders,
Thence to return as now we see them and
Ankle-deep in snow down the winter hill
Descend, while three birds watch and the fourth flies.

This scene from Brueghel, so perfectly rendered, exemplifies an aspect of Berryman's early work - - not its flaws, for quite simply it has none, but in the serenity, the absence of strain with which its style is subsumed into its subject. Indeed it is a poem so expressive of itself that nothing needs to be said about it. It resists commentary not by being superficial but with the uncluttered inclusiveness of the classic.

The same cannot be said of the lately published *Sonnets*, written in the 1940's and hitherto sensibly suppressed. As a sustained exercise in literary self-deception, they have a certain interest. What for the most part they reveal however is the poet we can be glad Berryman did not remain: the possessor of immense gifts who, not having found (or been discovered by) an adequate subject, surrenders to a diminishing convention. For the sonnets have no real subject, or rather the ostensible subject is not there. This is Allen Tate's "poetry of will" wrought to a pitch of virtually hysteric intensity. A very literary invention, the sonnet cycle perhaps inevitably invites a narcissistic performance.

> Troubling are masks . . . the faces of friends, my face
> Met unawares and your face: where I mum
> Your doubleganger writhes, wraiths are we come
> To keep a festival, none but wraiths embrace;
> Our loyal rite only we interlace,
> Laertes' winding sheet done and undone
> In Ithaca by day and night . . . we thrum
> Hopeful our shuffles, trusting to our disgrace.

This is every bit as unconvincing as Percy Shelley pretending to be Jacobean for the sake of the Cenci. The only genuine presence in these poems is that of the lover playing a role in which no reader can take him seriously, so limited and lacking in reciprocity is the image of the beloved. The lady, in short, is not merely insufficiently dramatized. She appears too clearly to exist only as a sounding board for an essentially self-indulgent psychic storm. The poet is here making a crisis out of literature, a reversal of the usual creative procedure that leads nowhere useful to poetry.

Bruno Bettelheim in *The Informed Heart* makes the point about compensating for gross pathology through intellectual or artistic achievement: "While lasting works of art may thus be created, those persons closest to the artist may be destroyed in the process" (p. 25). We may be drawn to speculate that in the Sonnets, pathology is not being accorded proper compensation. Literary credentials are perhaps being conferred upon it by regressive youth . . . to the detriment of poetry and truth as well.

In the *Dream Songs* Berryman has not ceased to be an exceedingly literary poet whose idiosyncracies have literary precedents. The *Dream Songs* are merely exceedingly literary poems pretending not to be. It is only fair to note that neither the literariness nor the anti-literariness here interferes with the compensatory art. The poet has found a means of liberating material which he cannot - - perhaps dare not - - fully understand: a predicament which the reader must share with him in a series of dream-like recognitions, in pity and joking fear.

Complex and ambitious (as sources of discovery rather than as structures), the *Dream Songs* are sustained by calculated risks, which may be interpreted as abdications of technique in favour of "style". The tension between subject matter and the style that contains it, typical of mannerism and probably an inevitable condition of American poetry now, is deliberately explored in its extremes. Like a prestidigitator, Berryman coaxes his revelations out of incongruous elements. He is testing the limits of expressiveness and he is doing so by drawing upon the ultimate resources of syntax rather than of language. For, though he ranges from the richly colloquial and even vulgar to the rhetorical and allusive, the purely musical, though he may on occasion employ words archaic or unusual enough to send readers to a dictionary (e.g. "in a foehn of loss"), his most conspicuous skill is in bringing these disparate elements into correspondence.

Huffy Henry hid the day,
unappeasable Henry sulked.
I see his point - - a trying to put things over.
It was the thought that they thought
they could do it made Henry wicked & away.
But he should have come out and talked.

All the world like a woolen lover
once did seem on Henry's side.
Then came a departure.
Thereafter nothing fell out as it might or ought.
I don't see how Henry, pried

open for all the world to see, survived.

What he has now to say is a long
wonder the world can bear & be.
Once in a sycamore I was glad
all at the top, and I sang.
Hard on the land wears the strong sea
And empty grows every bed.

In so far as they represent dreams, these poems wittily and movingly exploit the disjunctiveness, the arbitrariness, the comic disguises, the fictions that embody the deepest wishes and the discordances at work within the unconstrued areas of the mind. Henry, or Mr. Bones, figures here as the poet's alter ego and confidant. He resembles that ingenuously schizophrenic device out of childhood, the imaginary dompanion, to whom both fantasied exploits and misbehaviour could be attributed. In his honour the idiom of the stage darky is employed (a method of distancing that strikes some as untimely as it is precious). He serves to create tolerable diversions from painful material. Indeed, only with his assistance can otherwise inaccessible or intractable material find accommodation in the lyric mode.

The high ones die, die. They die. You look up and
who's there?
- - Easy, easy, Mr. Bones. I is on your side.
I smell your grief.
- - I sent my grief away. I cannot care
forever. With them all again & again I died
and cried, and I have to live.

- - Now there you exaggerate, Sah. We hafta die.
That is our 'pointed task. Love and die.

The wit and invention of these poems, especially in their mimetic extremes and in the sending up of clichés, is of a kind that very bright undergraduates strive for and rarely attain (or sustain). The Freudian quotient, the escape of impulse from the controlling censor, collaborates with highly conscious improvisation.

> Henry sats in de bar & was odd,
> off in the glass from the glass,
> at odds wif de world & its god,
> his wife is a complete nothing,
> St. Stephen
> getting even.
>
> . . .
>
> Henry's pelt was put on sundry walls
> where it did much resemble Henry and
> Them persons was delighted.
>
> . . .
>
> Turning it over, considering, like a madman
> Henry put forth a book.
> No harm resulted from this.

Such verbal tactics: the jokes, the fantasies, the ironies, the very simplifications of the comic gesture indicate the complexity of the poet's response to experience and effectively designate the emotional burden they contrive to mask. Offhandedness is indeed a signal of the troubled and troubling emotional center from which the poems derive. Witness "Henry's Confession":

> Nothin very bad happen to me lately.

How you explain that? - - I explain that, Mr. Bones,
terms o' your bafflin odd sobriety.
Sober as man can get, no girls, no telephones,
what could happen bad to Mr. Bones?
- - If life is a handkerchief sandwich,

in a modesty of death I join my father
who dared so long agone leave me.
A bullet on a concrete stoop
close by a smothering southern sea
spreadeagled on an island, by my knee.
- - You is from hunger, Mr. Bones,

I offers you this handkerchief, now set
your left foot by my right foot,
shoulder to shoulder, all that jazz,
arm in arm, by the beautiful sea,
hum a little, Mr. Bones.
- - I saw nobody coming, so I went instead.

These are nothing if not obsessively introspective poems, yet they are free of narcissism. Berryman's irony is virtually all toward himself ("We dream of honour, and we get along"). His wit is defensive. What it is defending is the privacy of the incommunicable, the primary experiences that we all have and cannot share. ("There sat down, once, a thing on Henry's heart / so heavy, if he had a hundred years / & more, & weeping, sleepless, in all them time / Henry could not make good.") The truth is that experiences of this order can be "made good" only in poems. According to the poem: "All the bells say: too late. This is not for tears; / thinking." By making a new experience out of the irremediable, the poem in some measure exorcizes that from which it arises. On the other hand, it is not difficult to detect from the tone and vocabulary instances of special pleading on the part of the poet using the wily tactics of the child in covert invitations to the world not only to forgive but to approve.

The syntax of all of us, even the second-hand and the subliterate, reflects the morphology of consciousness. Berryman's in its most whimsical elaborations is proof of a saving refusal to take himself too seriously, an unusual achievement for an American whose most distinguished (and puritan) contemporary is capable of soliciting our serious attention for a sore eye. The *Dream Songs* are a game Berryman is playing with reality - - perhaps a self-destructive game after all - - but they are not surrealist; automatic writing is not their method. If they are songs in a sense other than ironical, it is by reason precisely of being *composed*.

The refusal to stand on ceremony, the purposeful disappointment of contemporary readers' expectations of how poems ought to be written, characterizes our most significant post-Renaissance poets. Berryman belongs with Wyatt and Donne rather than Apollinaire. Their wit, intelligence and cheerful anarchy recurs in him. Yet it is ever the fate of innovators to create new conventions out of the bits and pieces of the old. The inexorable alexandrine had to be broken before the French could begin writing modern poetry, yet the revisionists tend to sound classic. What the *Dream Songs* tell us at this inauspicious moment of history is that there is nothing left out of which poetry can be made save the clichés and grammatical vagaries of the inarticulate, or the obsolete rhetoric of a departed age. Berryman chose both. The eccentric amalgam gives us back in purified intensity death and the fear of death, our common share.

Chapter Six

THE POETICS OF DISREGARD: HOMAGE TO BASIL BUNTING

Whatever habits of optimism have fortified our expectations of literature, probably none among us seriously imagines that any mute inglorious Audens or Lowells remain to be discovered. On the contrary, not a few of us would admit to wishing that an appreciable number of the indefatigable fraternity of poets-in-residence and circuit-riding bards would lapse into muteness. The muses deserve holidays like everyone else, but it seems that these uncritical wenches have in recent years between campus and Club Mediterranée, been more than ever misled into compromising attitudes rendering them and the verses they sponsor largely indistinguishable from all the other glib and narcissistic fantasies propagated in the world's centers of commerce. A certain disaccord seems implicit in the relations between a poet and the publisher who puts his work before an audience, the requisites of art and the motives of business being seldom and uneasily composed It was only to be expected in an age of transcendant hucksterism that the mass production of literary reputations would follow that of tooth paste, motor cars and move starlets with evolutionary inevitability.

But fame was an ambiguous quantity long before its manufacture became modernised. And recognition and fame were never properly transposable terms.

Reading the collected poems of Basil Bunting, a publication coinciding with this gentleman's seventieth birthday, has been a painfully mixed experience. For one's pleasure in encountering the richness and the rare integrity of his gifts is countered by a saddening awareness of the cultural impasse that for forty years permitted his neglect. If in the south of England, which is generally taken to be the cultural part, this had been an especially noteworthy period for poetry one could more readily find excuses for this injustice. But in view of the destitution certified by Pound (who himself gave up the thankless task - - recounted with despairing wit in *Mauberley* - - of rescuing English poetry from its self-willed mediocrity) what appears to be operating here is simply another instance of the death-wish.

Rome and the world would not ignore Catullus. The world is scarcely permitted to ignore various of our contemporaries manifestly less endowed. If Baudelaire himself had been born in a country other than France and nurtured upon other versions of Romanticism, would his rejection of them have so profoundly affected the course of poetry in languages other than his own? Or affected it at all? Would Miss Sitwell have contrived to overshadow him? Who does "discover" poets? The answer to this at least is evident. Poets are always discovered by other poets. It has never been otherwise. Critics, it must be admitted, make do with what they are given. What happens to those rare poets who fail to meet their peers? Who are not inclined to utilize the coattails of others? Who do not seek patronage or curry favour? Whatever occurs, a poet's development itself and not merely his career or external circumstances must be in some way modified.

The response of a poet to recognition when it comes to him, or to its absence when recognition ought to have come, tells us something of the human resources from which his art derives. If, as Valéry instructs us, "literature is the art of playing on the minds of others", then the absence of those disponible minds at certain stages of his development is a crippling deprivation for the poet. Few persons require fame, these frequently for shallow reasons indirectly related to their talents. The serious artist can live without approval, but he cannot well do without other minds to play upon, without - - to put it crudely - - adequate sounding boards. The indispensable solitude of the writer forces upon him a thoroughly familiar acquaintance with the workings of his own mind. For precisely this reason he is in greater need than others of the shaping aid of attention. Even if that attention should be reluctantly accorded or actively resisting, so long as it is intelligent, it is better than none at all.

Solipsism is not the least of the hazards to literature and yet solipsism is brought about by the very condition essential to the engendering of art. It is, one might say, more inevitable than fame and more reliable - - even necessary if we may count it, reflexively, as a kind of recognition. Thus fame should induce in the serious writer reservations, doubts, fear and further self-scrutiny, since it is all too likely to be merely the visible sign of antecedent compromise. (The invitation to "sell out" in this world comes early. The solipsist has not "sold out". His behaviour rather resembles "selling short".)

There are no compromises in this book: no competitive posturing for the benefit of a literary clique, none of the defenses of self pity or paranoia against the condition of the outsider. Forty years of going his own way have not diminished this poet's receptiveness to life, vitiated his sense of humor or precipitated a sterile retreat into sensibility at the expense of intelligence. Despite the interspersing silences - - many of the poems date from the twenties and early thirties, the forties and fifties are sparsely represented, the long and impressive "Briggflatts" is dated 1965 - - a vigorous consistency denotes this work. Every line of it was written by a poet in full command of his resources. Even the silences between poems bear the mark of authority. And silence is an art very difficult to practice. The successful poet's vanity has many opportunities to express itself in interim works. The only two living poets whose influence Bunting acknowledges, Zukovsky and Pound, have both written more copiously but not more scrupulously.

And Pound, even if he had not had to endure the indignity of imprisonment and the lunatic asylum, betrayed from his earliest (and to my mind best) period a lack of relatedness (does any human feeling assert itself before the Pisan Cantos?), a persistent paranoid stridency, the coercive omniscience of one who is convinced he is incapable of error. Generosity is a notably uncommon phenomenon among men of letters. Yet, whatever the vicissitudes of Mr. Bunting's life on four continents (I understand only by report that it has entailed poverty on an Orwellian scale) frustration did not become his theme or the human race his target rather than his study.

Like others before him who have worked in isolation, he has found his true contemporaries in books. He states in his preface, "If ever I learned the trick of it, it was mostly from poets long dead whose names are obvious: Wordsworth and Dante, Horace, Wyatt and Malherbe, Manuchehri and Ferdosi, Villon, Whitman, Edmund Spenser." If there were not this wide, eclectic and well-assimilated influence behind these poems, I might have limited myself to suggesting that the revolution has been essentially a Catullan revolution. For his forceful masculinity, density of line and colloquial stance are distinctly of this order. But his range is greater, his relations to his subjects less egocentric and his music more subtly articulated.

As early as 1925 in "Villon", the first poem in the book and one of a group termed sonatas, this mastery is apparent. I quote from the third and concluding "movement". From the prison scene of the preceding sections we shift here to a prospect of history, a meditation in visual, tactile and spatial terms on the experience of temporality, located for us under the olive trees on green terraces where the sea beyond becomes a part of the perspective:

where it ravelled and spun
graveclothes of men

Romans and modern men
and the men of the sea
who have neither nation nor time. . .

The observer sees the shrines of the goddess of the country, the offerings, and below him the ports:

shipless spoiled sacked
because of the beauty of Helen
precision clarifying vagueness;
boundary to a wilderness
of detail; chisel voice
smoothing the flanks of noise;
catalytic making whisper and whisper
run together like two drops of quicksilver;
factor that resolves
            unnoted harmonies;
name of the nameless;
            stuff that clings
to frigid limbs
            more marble hard
than girls imagined by Mantegna. . .
The sea has no renewal, no forgetting,
no variety of death.
is silent with the silence of a single note.
How can I sing with my love in my bosom?
Unclean, immature and unseasonable salmon.

The virtues of this simple passage are more than Latin. That Pound is his master is apparent, yet even more apparent from a perusal of the Odes that follow - - vivid and astringent Englishings of the poet's "spoils" from the Persian Rudaki, Several lines in "Briggflatts" praising Scarlatti who condensed so much music into so few bars with never a crabbed turn or congested cadence, never a boast or a see-here describe his own results with perfect accuracy. To achieve them he has resorted to tactics available "before the rules made poetry a pedant's game", namely from Old English, a poetry deriving from a long oral tradition and filled with a forceful mnemonic vocal Mr. Bunting is himself Northumbrian, the vocabulary of his poem runic in its simplicity, a speech pungently spoken. The same interest that led Hopkins to devise sprung rhythms has led Bunting to explore the tonal relations of an all but uninflected tongue. His is a poetry above all to be heard. In fact, a record of Bunting reading "Briggflatts" was made in England, not un-obtainable, it seems. The following sample will meanwhile suggest the remarkable sensory sharpness that goes with the music.

A mason times his mallet
to a lark's twitter,
listening while the marble rests.
lays his rule
at a letter's edge,
fingertips checking,
till the stone spells a name
naming none.
a man abolished.
Painful lark, labouring to rise!
The solemn mallet says:
In the grave's slot
he lies. We rot.

Decay thrusts the blade,
wheat stands in excrement
trembling. Rawthey trembles.
Tongue stumbles, ears err
for fear of spring.
Rub the stone with sand,
wet sandstone rending
roughness away. Fingers
ache on the rubbing stone.

The mason says: Rocks
happen by chance.
No one here bolts the door,
love is so sore.

A kind of autobiography, "but not a record of fact", "Briggflatts" runs to over seven hundred lines in five substantial parts terminating in a short coda. The sense of life it conveys is transmitted by powers of observation so acute as to assume a riddling mimetic intensity:

I am neither snake nor lizard,
I am the slowworm.

Ripe wheat is my lodging. I polish
my side on pillars of its transept,
gleam in its occasional light.
Its swaying
copies my gait.

"Briggflatts" takes its name from a remote village near the river Rawthey in West Riding, Yorkshire not far from Westmoreland where a seventeenth century Quaker Meeting House stands amid a cluster of old cottages, oak and chestnut trees. The Meeting House in fact shares the stone roof of a neighboring cottage. A guidebook to this region describes the place: "Through a tiny porch and a fine old door with over 100 oak pegs we step into a room of days gone by, very quaint with its few plain benches, walls with simple panelling, and a gaited stairway to the gallery. With Winder and Home Fell towering above it on two sides, the little garden is shaded by cypress, oak, and a spreading yew. At the Meeting House is treasured a fragment of a yew tree under which George Fox is said to have preached when he came to Sedburgh."

"Briggflatts" is addressed to the memory of a young girl loved by the poet from whom he was separated by his imprisonment as a conscientious objector during the 1914 War. The poet's return to this place and to the emotions it holds for him reminds us forcibly of Eliot's curious and touching meditation in *Burnt Norton* upon what might have been. Yet the differences between the harsh, wild, lonely and abandoned landscape of Garsdale and the cultivated rectangles, the soft inhabited countryside of the Cotswolds are borne out in the two poems and are in each case analogous to the quality of the emotions evoked: Active nostalgia on the one hand and passive nostalgia on the other. For, whereas we are not in doubt of the real person whose existence is celebrated in the present tense in Mr. Bunting's poem ("My love is young but wise. Oak, applewood, / her fire is banked with ashes till day. / The fells reek of her hearth's scent. . .") the ghostly voices of Mr. Eliot's children in the garden are more problematically the voices of children unbegotten by the poet, who wrote his poems instead.

A poet so fascinated with the aspects of tone color, with the sounds his verses make, runs the risk of emptying content of another order out of his poem, or attenuating it as usually happens in song. This is not an accident that has ever befallen Mr. Bunting. Indeed, form and content have perhaps never been more consubstantial. Read "The Orotava Road", "The Well of Lycopolis", "Vestiges", "How Duke Valentine Contrived" (an assortment of murders according to Machiavelli), or any of the Odes at random and you will see what this means.

Finally, though we live in a century prolific in translations, where poetry is concerned this is often merely a matter of priming the pump (pony in hand). Rarely does translation become a creative act of appropriation by which a poet comes more fully to grips with his own conscience as maker. Mr. Bunting has ransacked world literature in the most profitable way possible to himself and to us. As early as 1932 he came across the venerable Kamo-no-Chomei (born at Kamo 1154, died at Toyama on Mount Hino, 24 June 1216) by means of the Italian Professor Muccioli's version of the latter's journals, making out of the old man's recollections a long elegiac poem such as Chomei himself might have done had the infirmities of age not intervened. It is one of the best things in the book.

Chomei, it seems, was a civil servant, poet, and writer of critical essays. Turned down for a desired job in a Shinto temple, he "next day announced his conversion to Buddhism". He retired from public life after helping to compile the Imperial Anthology, installed himself in a mountain cottage and wrote his memoirs, evidently urbane, ironical, unembittered, with all the sadness unstated.

When I get bored with this place.
Two barrowloads of junk
and the cost of a man to shove the barrow,
no trouble at all
. . .
I sit at the window with a headful of old verses.
Whenever a money howls there are tears on my cuff.

Little enough to suggest the flavor of a 320 line poem with fires, floods, earthquakes, domestic history and philosophy in it. Enough perhaps to hint at the shifts of tone that disclose a complex, compassionate, disinterested and benevolent mind.

So long as the practice of literature in England by original and independent outsiders remains as embarrassing as vice, and the endorsement of mediocrity a motivating factor of cultural life, Basil Bunting may continue with every reason for tranquility of mind to ply the poetics of disregard. England does not deserve him: the only worthy successor to Hopkins - - who also had to wait.

Chapter Seven

THE TRANSLATOR AS POET

If "the memory of gratification is at the origin of all thinking, and the impulse to recapture past gratification is the hidden driving power behind the process of thought" as Marcuse suggests *(Eros and Civilization,* p. 29), then perhaps the most charitable explanation for the characteristic Anglo-American chauvinism that extends in our universities to a fear of the Foreign in literature is to be found in our commonly advertized incapacity for languages. The recoil of the mind from work that is painful, baffling and ungratifying explains to some extent the peculiar quality of English intellectual life. Doubtless the Puritan reflex, the ground-bass as it were of Anglo-American experience, adds a further kink to this response to bafflement so typically expressed as renunciations of cleverness. Such, at any rate, is the distrust of works in translation reflected in our syllabi, it seems that many of us would prefer that our undergraduates read any kind of rubbish - - so long as it is British Rubbish - - rather than a single masterpiece in translation. Reading Foreign books might be

And the voice of Conscience supplies a clerical censor that warns: in changing all those words over from one language to another Mistakes Can Be Made. Men of little imagination, it must be admitted, by reason of their lesser ductility of mind disqualify themselves from responding adequately to those "mistakes" integral to artistic expression.

If one is addicted to literature one even comes to value those imperfections in our masterpieces that no one but a lover would notice: not only Flaubert's errors in arithmetic in settling thebill for a broken leg, or discrepancies in the Yonville-Rouen stagecoach schedule, but the occasional "inconsistency in matters of feeling" as well from Lermentov to Stendhal that, Tolstoy attests in his *Childhood*, "is the surest sign of their genuineness." I am touching upon a matter that Mr. Ransom has already been taken to task for describing as the texture of irrelevance in poetry. Perhaps no poem differs more from another than it does from itself in another translation. Yet even this difference ought not to be despised because, however imperfect, it *is* a bridge instead of an abyss. Moreover, with Valéry masquerading as the Virgil of the *Bucolics* on my side, I am convinced that "fidelity to meaning alone is a kind of betrayal" and that distortions of the greatest magnitude are the result of mere accuracy in translation.

Into the most conscious art an element of the gratuitous enters. Nowhere is this gratuitous element more likely to be felt than at the point of origin of the poem. But whether in the shape of inspiration or under the pressure of more clearly defined experience, these data are not only anterior to, but qualitatively different from the poem itself. Moreover, the poem that ensues differs essentially from the experience which prompted it even if the experience in which it originated was purely verbal. The poem itself is a new experience. The same cannot fail to be true of a poem in translation. This being so, why should this uniqueness provide occasion for regret in the case of translation when we would not think of lamenting literal-mindedly the lost consonance between the poem in its inception and its final articulation?

Imprudent distinctions, no doubt, in the context of our present cultural confusion when ignorance of a language no longer constitutes a deterrent to many a translator. The ideal translator I have in mind would gravitate easily into Pound's classification of mastery, as attentive to the possibilities of words as a good carpenter to the grain of different kinds of wood. In short, a poet of considerable competence. Mr. Nims in fact, whose book *From Sappho to Valéry* I wish to discuss, seems to me a conscientious representative of this class. Only at this level, needless to say, can the "mistakes" I have advocated transcend mere sloppy mindedness and attain an heuristic function, revealing perhaps what the author of the original might not have realized he had to say.

Ezra Pound of course is the great grandaddy of such creative translation in English, and his influence - - even upon himself - - has given rise to inconsistencies most readers will feel several ways about. Whatever our response to the more repellant features of Pound's notions, features that may be detected at least in embryo (typographical) from his earliest published remarks, these fixed attitudes, the arrogance, the willfulness, the contempt are unalterably intermixed with other qualities altogether admirable, including a completely selfless dedication to poetry and imaginative gifts probably superior to any of his contemporaries'. His was, however, an untrained mind and a radically ineducable one. Yet if he has been paranoid he has had something to be paranoid about. If an intransigent American optimism displaced in him the ordinary function of consecutive thought, his tragedy lay in having nothing whatever to be optimistic about. But even those who saw him as "a barbarian on the loose in a museum" recognized in Pound the qualities of a great translator. What was needed to recover Propertius, the Seafarer, Li Po, Cavalcanti and company from the hands of the philologists and the encrustations of time was exactly this "rich and disordered memory" - - memory and that language which is memory's gift. In Whitehead's words: ". . . an articulated memory is the gift of language considered as an expression from oneself in the past to oneself in the present,"[1] a history that consists, in the now virtually complete work of Pound, exclusively in an art of surfaces. For the difficulty with Pound has always been that nothing lay discoverable beneath the crafted surfaces of his texts. Nothing connected; everything juxtaposed.

One may in the human scheme see immense pathos in the unloving and unlovably obsessive spectacle of impersonation, the literary - - and often shallowly literary - - adoption of surrogate emotion on the part of an artist who evidently had no identity, no mind, no feeling of his own, merely a frustrated ego and a viable sensibility. But we must honour such defenses insofar as they represent successful attacks on the language of the tribe, raids upon the inarticulate for us all.

> Persephone and Dis, Dis, have mercy upon her,
> These are enough women in hell, quite enough beautiful
> women
> Iope, and Tyro, and Pasiphae, and the formal girls of
> Achaia,
> And out of the Troad, and from the Campania,
> Death has his tooth in the lot, Averaus lusts for the lot
> of them,
> Beauty is not eternal, no man has perennial fortune,
> Slow foot, or swift foot, death delays but for a season.

Pound's persona speaks a quasi-colloquial, unadorned and wholly invented idiom the basic unit of which is the simple declarative statement. Gravity and irony are not here in obvious competition but the implicit doubleness haunts the reader, or at least this reader, without the implementation of rhetorical pointing to which a lesser poet would resort. In an earlier mode, while only just avoiding the Tennysonian and the Miltonic, Pound tended to achieve rather fake antique effects. Goeth - falleth, knoweth - recalleth, floweth - palleth, gloweth - befalleth, showeth - calleth, gloweth - falleth, moweth - calleth all occur in the (rejected) "Canzon: Of Incense" of Arnaut Daniel. But the pre-Raphaelite pose was too languid to support a more ambitious art and Mauberley is both the incarnation and the exorcism of that phase of Pound's development, a quite convincing laying of his own youthful putative ghost. The more fully Pound was able to disappear into his persona, to assume the identity of another poet, to lose his own bullying and abrasive mannerisms, the more spare, clear, supple and authentic the verse becomes. The Pound who enunciated "Poetry ought to be at least as well written as prose" himself wrote characteristically hectoring, bombastic, careless, unpolished, brutally dictatorial prose. Those arrogant paranoid protestations on the topic of the imbecility of the world's conduct toward poets certainly do not enlist the tragic imagination. But the Propertius who intones:

> Shades of Callimachus, Coan ghosts of Philetas,
> It is in your grove I would walk
> I who come first from the clear font
> Bringing the Grecian orgies into Italy,
>   and the dance into Italy.
> Who hath taught you so subtle a measure,
>   in what hall have you heard it;
> What foot beat out your time-bar,
>   what water has mellowed your whistles?
>
> Out-weariers of Apollo will, as we know, continue their Martian generalities,
>   We have kept our erasers in order.
> A new-fangled chariot follows the flower-hung horses;
> A young Muse with young loves clustered about her
>   ascends with me into the aether, . . .
> And there is no high-road to the Muses.

for these "few pages brought down from the forked hill unsullied" earns the wreath of our committed attention.

But Pound, lost in his own *machismo*, is quite incapable of imagining himself into the character of a woman. Hence his construction of Daianeira in his *Women of Trachis* as a sort of George Cracker ("Looks are my trouble") - undifferentiated as to intellect and unmotivated by passion - further obscures an already problematical play. Having retreated from his earlier tendency to the antique, Pound seems here to have gone so far to rectify that failing that his desperately breezy colloquialism is already bizarrely dated. To readers acquainted with the spare simplicity of the original, Pound's ingenuity seems an intolerable vandalism. H.A. Mason's discerning and detailed reading (*Cambridge Quarterly*, vol. 4, 1969) is surely the most useful and fair to both authors. What such exertions on the part of Pound *and* the scholars suggest so late in his career is that judgment has never become Pound's strong point. He is at his best in submitting to the superior tact of a mature artist but invariably false in his personal intrusions even into his own poems. The rather crude social vignettes to be found in the Cantos, for example, could not by any stretch of the imagination be conceived high points of that enterprise. Understandably less sympathetic is the misguided inspiration to supplant Sophocles with an amalgam of uncle Ezra's homemade jargon.

A far happier (and well documented) influence is that of the troubadour and Tuscan poets. Quite simply they civilized Pound. Even the bellicose Bertrans de Born, by supplying the occasion for acting out aggression ("Damn it all! all this our South stinks peace.") must have helped neutralize Pound's perpetual high dudgeon. The dazzling technique of the Provençal poets provided Pound with the best part of his content for years to come. They taught him nearly everything he needed to learn about the musical principle of language, and the advice he formulated for others was equally and drastically true of his own work: "poetry withers and 'dries out' when it leaves music, or at least an imagined music, too far behind it." Music alone, it could be argued, allowed Pound to write poems or passages of poetry of the first intensity. The impressionist drift, the absence of argument, all that assisted in the process of representation without the foreclosing rictus of "thought" lent assurance and grace to a performance that was capable at any moment of turning into harangue.

Palace in smoky light,
Troy but a heap of smouldering boundary stones,
ANAXIFORMINGES! Aurunculeia!
Hear me. Cadmus of Golden Prows!
The silver mirrors catch the bright stones and flare,
Dawn, to our waking, drifts in the green cool light;
Dew-Haze blurs, in the grass, pale ankles moving.
Beat, Beat, whirr, thud, in the soft turf
            under the apple trees,

Choros nympharum, goat-foot, with the pale foot alternate;
Crescent of blue-shot waters, green-gold in the shallows,
A black cock crows in the sea foam;

And by the curved, carved foot of the couch,
            claw-foot and lion head, an old man seated
Speaking in the low drone . . . -
            Ityn!
Et ter flebiliter, Itys, Ityn!
And she went toward the window and cast her down,
            'All the while, the while, swallows crying:
Ityn!
            'It is Cabestan's heart in the dish.'
            'It is Cabestan's heart in the dish?'
            'No other taste shall change this.'

Professor Nims extends his range and ours in a volume of seventy-one poems by twenty poets in nine languages: Catalan, Provençal, French, German, Galician, Spanish, Greek, Latin and Italian, handsomely presented with original texts and their translations on facing pages. The most interesting of these is the Catalan poet Ausias March, a feudal lord of the early fifteenth century who, after youthful tours of duty under Alfonso the Magnanimous in Sardinia, Corsica, Naples, Sicily and Africa, settled in his native Valencia to produce a body of work strangely modern in its reflection of a disturbed and disturbing consciousness and quite revolutionary in its rejection of the conventions and diction of the troubadour poets, his predecessors. He has been compared to Donne and Baudelaire, and Professor Nims, noting the tension between love in its sexual and spiritual aspects that informs the poems, likens him to an impolite Petrarch, "unmusical, abrupt, infuriated" and calls attention to the violent, concentrated, richly and colloquially metaphorical qualities of his language. Like Dante, March was the first to write poetry in his native Catalan instead of the literary language sanctioned by tradition. Some two hundred lines in translation offer an incomparable inducement to the study of Catalan. Although Nims' lines do not seem to me quite to reflect the jagged, violent concentration of the divided consciousness he attributes to March - - whoever he is translating, Nims' bouncy and irrepressible boyishness prevails - - ("Joy at the door tells Sorrow: This way in.") but nevertheless a clear enough representation of the issue of the "long infirmity of love" tells us that only an artist of the first rank could have produced it.

Equally attractive and no less challenging in the difficulties with which the texts bristle for the translator are the twelfth century *Chansons d'Amour* of Bernard de Ventadorn from which Nims offers a generous selection. A more joyful fellow than most of his contemporaries, Bernart, I would guess, comes closest to expressing the natural temperament of his translator. Admittedly Nims is aiming to retrieve these verses for the speaking voice rather than the singing voice that is the chief excuse of Provençal poetry, but anyone who has glanced at the originals or laboured himself over the rendering of a single stanza will readily appreciate the *tour de force* these versions represent. Nims' Bernart:

> God, girl, we're getting nowhere fast in love!
> Time's running out, a stuff we've little of.
> Let's deal in codes and hidden winks; we could
> work by finesse, if being brave's no good.
>
> A lover's in the right to blame
> a lady who excuses, balks;
> makes love a conversation game
> and talks and talks. And talks and talks.
> You can love here, and elsewhere say you do;
> tell a fine lie when none's to check on you.
>
> Lady, receive your lover! Then you'll learn
> How I can lie and lie to serve your turn.
>
> Messenger, here's the message. Let her know
> how - - with this pounding pulse - - I'd quake to go.

Rosalia de Castro, another of the "linguistically underprivileged" poets to whom Nims attends, is one of the most sympathetic and without a doubt also one of the greatest. How much Keats might have learned from her! Celtic longing and Sapphic restraint appear unerringly combined in her simple unaffected lines, close both to folk speech and folk song in her native Galician. A contemporary of Emily Dickinson, her work is both softened and sharpened by its truthfulness to unspeculative sense.

Nims' effect on Valéry is subtly unsophisticating. Once again a delightfully high spirited adolescent comes through whose tones one has not detected in the French, but which one concludes by finding an acceptable alternative. What looks and sounds as easy as falling off a log in fact is the result of well-concealed and highly professional work resulting in density without congestion and without metrical impediment. Here is Nims' rendering of the final stanza of Valéry's Marine Cemetery poem:

The freshening wind! Let's live, or try to! Look
The vast air ruffles and claps shut my book;
Reckless, the surf goes geysering on the rocks.
Sun-spangled pages, dazzled, blow away!
Waves, shatter! Shatter in a jubilant spray
This quiet roof where jabbed the focc'sle flocks.

Somehow Goethe had never struck me as a charming poet either. In Professor Nims' translating he becomes so. And Catallus turns out to be a nice guy, probably from Chicago, who would never for a moment have taken himself too seriously. *Sappho to Valéry* is a personal anthology in the best sense, from which anyone who cares for poetry may derive lasting enjoyment and those who write it may learn to take pleasure in the work.

Knowing only one's own langauge, if one is a poet, is never enough. And poets writing in English, especially Canadian and American poets whose often unconscious nationalism can only warp and impoverish their work - - these above all need to know that the others exist, and how they are solving the problems only poets can teach one another how to solve. While the admiration of his peers can easily retard a poet's development, the tutelage of his betters - - wherever they are to be found - - is something no poet can go without. This is a prayer for them. Amen.

FOOTNOTES

1. A.N. Whitehead, *Modes of Thought*, p. 46.

Chapter Eight

AN ADJUNCT TO THE POET'S DOSSIER

Ovid, who rewards the reader with such profusion and variety in his *Metamorphoses*, is the only poet of durable influence that I can call to mind whose very gifts have been held against him. It happens often enough that a poet's worst enemies are his most fervent admirers, using his coattails when they are incapable of invention, and dimming the memory of his authentic accomplishment with inept imitation. Ovid has not suffered at the hands of poets. We may, with Francis Meres be content that "the sweet witty soul of Ovid" lives on in Shakespeare without for a moment doubting that he lives on as well, transmuted, in Petrarch, Boccaccio, Marlowe, Drayton, Davydd ap Gwilym, Milton, Goethe, Ezra Pound . . . or Picasso. The uses to which he has been put by artists are such that any poet would welcome and should enhance rather than impair his reputation. Perhaps the greatest test of his resilience was to have survived the admiration of the Middle Ages, for so potent and addictive were his attractions then that the Fathers of the Church were driven to disingenuous lengths to moralize him into Christian respectability. But whereas poets and theologians have been unafflicted with doubts in his regard, scholars - - who frequently suffer from a sort of sensibility lag - - have tended to bring ponderous Romantic expectations to their scrutiny of the texts. Ovid, too clever by half, was not serious enough for them. Furthermore, until Ovid, they had been able to take comfort in the Latin poets' orderly habit of employing certain meters for certain kinds of subjects - - and sticking to them in the prescribed manner for whole books at a time. The *Metamorphoses* disconcerted them at the outset by a quasi-elegiac and wholly novel use of the epic meter. Inevitably, those who were deluded enough to see Catullus as "the tenderest of the Roman poets" could be expected to find Ovid "heartless", a qualification that, properly understood, ought to go a long way toward rehabilitating him for modern audiences. The palpable, though unstated, scholarly regrets that Ovid had not chosen to be a second-rate Vergil have a pathos that Ovid himself would have found amusing - - rather like wishing that a greyhound had elected to imitate a Saint Bernard.

The efforts of scholars to be definitive about our classics more reliably elucidate the critical preconceptions of the periods they exemplify than the works of the authors to which they are attached. Thus the critical consensus that for so many years found Ovid "frivolous" (Savonarola went so far as to think the *Metamorphoses* the work of a madman) may be seen to express nothing so much as the fear of fun and the distrust of laughter. It is not Ovid who is naive but his detractors, whose defective sense of humor represents the greatest impediment to penetrating his "cool".

What Ovid's *Metamorphoses* illustrate with extraordinary aplomb and finesse is not the inability to commit himself to a judgment of his materials, often attributed with self-congratulatory moral opprobrium to the writer who is *degage*, but rather the imaginative capacity to sustain multiple points of view, the perception of diverse planes of reality that signifies the rare artist. Nor is the narrative continuity of the *Metamorphoses* vitiated by the poet's promiscuous disinclination to concentrate his drams within a limited and confined point of view. The essence of Ovid's technical address lies in the very abruptness and momentum of these daring shifts. In this he is expressing a complexity of attitude very different from having no attitude at all, as well as a species of that absorption with the sources of human behaviour that motivates those modern artists whom we most admire, the proof of whose compassion rests precisely in the detachment with which they practice it. For the sympathetic imagination is no more dissociated from the analytical in Ovid's poem than it is in Henry James' *The Golden Bowl.*

Nor to the instances of authorial intrusion in the narrative indicate any sacrifice of this essential aesthetic distancing. Homer and Vergil intrude rarely in their epics so that when they do so we are aware that an important moment has come. Ovid enters his narratives habitually but with such unobtrusive point, securing an astringent and often witty distance from the scene, that the dramatic outcome resembles the alienation effect of a Brechtian performance. The poet controls our response in such a manner that our attention is not deflected from the action to the narrator, but so focussed as to collaborate with him in criticizing and appraising the events or, more often, the psychological motives of which the events are compacted, rather than nursed to succumb passively to an illusionist panorama. Ovid is nothing if not dramatic, then, and attention has often been called to this flair of his, yet neither is he confined to the cumbersome machinery or static space of the theatre. Above all, in his mobility and his absolute freedom to assume a continually shifting perspective of the action, he is surely cinematic.

Readers whose experience attending films has accustomed them to the unexpected: to the abrupt transitions, sophisticated cutting, the disjunctive and counterpointed metaphorical reference of cinema graphics as handled by those directors we like to call poetic, such readers have the best possible preparation for appreciating Ovid. A style is a style; it will have its own procedures, its own rhetoric, its mannerisms, it will always represent a state of mind, a way of seeing as well as shaping its materials. Yet ultimately not many artists - - among them Ovid preeminently - - are able to make of their medium something transparent as a window or a screen through which we survey in panels or in moving "shots" the intense visual texture of a reality felt but perhaps never encountered elsewhere so vividly except in fleeting dreams. If we have seen the films of Vigo, Franju, Brunuel, Bresson or Wajda, to name a few, we shall scarcely interpret Ovid's impressionistic concentration on the *mise-en-scène* as superficial, Ovid's ironies as a betrayal of seriousness, Ovid's use of the grotesque as sadistic, or Ovid's jokes as a failure to estimate the tragic potential of life.

*

Actaeon, having blundered inadvertently upon Diana and her nymphs bathing, suffers the rather extreme consequences of offended virginity by being changed into a stag, hunted down and killed by his own hounds. Ovid, clearly fascinated by the feeling we have of being contained within our bodies without perhaps being entirely defined by them, prolongs our scrutiny of the transformation, dwelling characteristically on its most ambiguous moments when the transformee is neither quite one thing nor the other. (I quote from the wonderful George Sandys translation of 1632, recently made available in a fine edition by the University of Nebraska Press.)

> Shee side-long turnes, looks back, and wisht her bow:
> Yet, what she had, she in his face did throwe,
> With vengefull Waters sprinkled; to her rage
> These words shee addes, which future Fate presage:
> Now, tell how thou hast seene me disarray'd;
> Tell if thou canst: I give thee leave. This said,
> Shee to his neck and eares new length imparts;
> This Browe the antlers of long-living Harts:
> His leggs and feet with armes and hands supply'd;
> And cloth'd his body in a spotted hide.
> To this, feare added. Autonoeus flyes,
>
> And wonders at the swiftness of his thighes,
> But, when his looks he in the River view'd,

> He would have cry'd, Woe's me, No words insew'd:
> His words were grones. He frets, with galling teares,
> Cheeks not his owne; yet his owne mind he beares.
> What should he doe? Goe home? or in the Wood
> For ever lurke? Feare, this; shame that withstood.

Even while these doubts mingle with the strange timidity of his new condition, his own dogs, all identified by name and not in the least uncertain of their proper roles, take up the chase. His friends, cheering on the pack, call to the missing Actaeon to joint the sport:

> He (too neare!)
> Made answer by mute motions, blam'd of all
> For being absent at his present fall.

The dogs close in to seize a quarry wracked by human thoughts, human tears streaming from animal eyes, unable to summon a human voice in its last conscious act.

Daphne in full flight from Apollo's pressing courtship reaches her father's river and prays for rescue. In a quasi-sexual torpor she finds herself changing into a laurel tree. Apollo, touching the bark, can feel her human heart still beating within, and when he attempts an embrace the branches recoil.

Io spends an unconscionably long time in the shape of a heiffer, but is nonetheless readily recognized in this form by her father on a chance meeting. Of course she is capable of jotting messages down with her hoof. On the other hand, she is charmingly reticient about resuming human speech after the Argus has been slain and her imprisonment ended, lest an inappropriate lowing should occur.

Salmacis the water nymph simply disappears into her own medium, subsumed into the bisexual identity of Hermaphroditus.

The mad wanderings and final mutation of the weeping Byblis into a fountain merely represent the last stages of a closely observed psychic metamorphosis, a disintegration initiated by her rationalization of an unrealisable incestuous passion. The reunion of Ceyx and Alcyone to live out their legend of faithfulness as birds suggests less the deprivation of humanity than provision for a superadded freedom.

Dream material, certainly, drawing upon our reserves of guilt as well as the wish-fulfilling resources of our fantasy. What adult reader in this age that specializes in crises of identity, could fail to be affected by such transformations? Yet, if reading Ovid is more satisfying than dreaming, it must be because he is equally able to represent the mutuality of stable relations as well as the destructive power of excessive or misplaced passion.

Now that, from the vantage point of the worst century so far, we can see what Romanticism has come to, we can appreciate the inaccuracy of the Romantic attribution of "soullessness" to Ovid. Because his career was not devoted to the advertisement of his soul, because he failed to impose himself with a certain imperialism upon the reader, his invitation to the translator and to the magpie instincts of the poets, has proved all the stronger. Nor would it be an exaggeration to say that the translation of Ovid, a Renaissance industry, contributed substantively to the perfection of the closed couplet in English. Among these early translations, that of Sandys, already mentioned, is undoubtedly the best and historically of greater interest even than Dryden's. Sandys' concision (for which Dryden once reproached him) obviously is the result of more than mere work. One of those seemingly legendary Renaissance types who could turn their hands effortlessly and stylishly to almost anything, a serious traveler who wrote a much admired account of his visits to Turkey, Egypt, Italy and the Holy Land, Sandys composed his version of Ovid in America, apparently working at it by night (in between Indian raids), for his full working days were occupied with the affairs of the Vriginia Colony's treasury. I regret that the present edition of a work so worth owning should be so expensive. (Poor Ovid, shivering in his Rumanian exile, should have had the consolation of this kind of revenue.)

Arthur Golding's translation of 1567 is better known, but mainly for its exuberant eccentricity. His ungainly fourteeners, extravagantly admired though they were by Pound, afford every delight except that of poetry. Golding's version is several thousand lines longer than Ovid's, a diffuseness contrasting significantly with the precision and condensation that so recommend Sandys. Golding begins, as his latest editor J.F. Nims says, by metamorphosing Ovid and this transformation of the Augustan mannerist into an Elizabethan rustic is so enchanting on its own account that no one's library should be without a copy. A prototypical example of woman's lib reads in Golding's version:

> And Scylla beateth on theyr ryght: which from the navell downe
> Is patched up with cruell curres: and upward to the crowne
> Dooth keepte the countnance of a mayd, and (if that all be trew
> That Poets fayne) shee was sumtyme a mayd ryght fayre of hew.
> To her made many wooers sute: all which shee did eschew.
> And going to the salt Sea nymphes (to whom shee was ryght deere)
> She vaunted, to how many men shee gave the slippe that yeare.

None of the modern translations quite achieves this flavour, the result of ignoring the *faux-naif* in Ovid and supplying an abundant measure of the translator's own unassailable simplicity. Among the modern renditions, that of Rolfe Humphries is well known but I think less successful because the blank verse line within which he chose to work lacks the tautness, the quick, light movement of the original. (I should like to digress to the extent of mentioning Humphries' translation of the little known Welsh metaphysical poet, Dafydd ap Gwilym, an Ovidian contemporary of Chaucer, whose *Nine Thorny Thickets* deserves to be more widely appreciated. Mr. Humphries' version posthumously published by the Kent State University Press, is a beautiful example of book design, containing as well a musical setting of the title poem composed by Johnny Mercer.)

If a third volume of the *Metamorphoses* on one's shelves does not seem unduly obsessive. A.E. Watts' excellent version, published together with the etchings of Picasso by the University of California Press, may well offer the most immediate and agreeable entry to the poem. Mr. Watts, a distinguished translator of Propertius as well, appreciates Ovid's unpretentious, almost throwaway method of exploiting literary conventions. This rapid, light, clear, plastic, and effortlessly sustained performance captures most adequately for the modern ear what Professor Brooks Otis of Stanford has called the polytonality of Ovid. Here is a passage from the story of Proserpine, Pluto's child bride, whose rescue from the underworld was thwarted by the sneaky tale-bearer, metamorphosed below, who saw her break the prescribed fast.

His speech left Ceres fixed in her intent
To fetch her, but the fates withheld consent.
Proserpin's fast was broken, for below
In goodly orchards, where pongranates grow,
She strayed and plucked, unthinking, pleased to find
The seeds enclosed within the yellow rind,
Seven seeds she crushed, and none was there to see
Save Orphne's son Ascalaphus, whom she
Of nymphs Avernian not the most unknown,
Had borne in darkling woods to Acheron.

He saw and told in mere malevolence,
And stopped her by his take returning thence.
She sighed with grief, the captive queen of hell;
And on the informer soon her anger fell;
As, dashed with drops of Phlegethon, his face
To beak and plumes and monstrous eyes gave place.
Robbed of himself, in alien garb he goes,
With tawny wings and talon-bearing toes.
His arms go slack, and growing all to head,
He scarce has strength his new-born wings to spread;
And so he ends, a loathed, unsightly fowl,
Prophet of woe to men, a skulking owl.

He has, I think, the look of a scholar of the very sort that has given the negative drift to Ovid's dossier. But who wants to be the favorite poet of all those people who never read books? One does not have to be a schoolboy to adore Ovid, the cleverest poet in the world, of whose fund of cleverness poetry stands in deeper need than ever.

Chapter Nine

THE CONSUMMATION OF CONSCIOUSNESS: THE POETRY OF DELMORE SCHWARTZ

A contemporary of John Berryman, Robert Lowell and Randall Jarrell, equally gifted, yet in his gifts more vulnerable than they, Delmore Schwartz is a recent instance of the fatality of poetry. Because his work - - in part so nearly perfect, in part badly flawed - - represents an effort of survival (much like that of Kafka), of exorcising in the aesthetic realm an irremediable psychic disturbance, any account we attempt of it would appropriately consider the relation of these tensions to the act of poetry. The poet is dead; the personal devastation, the existential cost we can mourn and respect. The poems endure uniquely to console and to accuse, their mode of existence apt for analysis.

In *Eros and Civilization* Harbert Marcuse reminds us that "Art is perhaps the most visible 'return of the repressed', not only on the individual but also on the generic-historical level. The artistic imagination shapes the 'unconscious memory' of the liberation that failed, of the promise that the cathartic effect of art epitomizes the dual function of art: both to oppose and to reconcile; both to indict and to acquit; both to recall the repressed and to repress it again - 'purified'."[1] Among the early poems of Schwartz are paired two that enact the Hegelian contention of opposites to which the poet's mind responds with painful intensified awareness. They are: "For the One Who Would Take Man's Life in His Hands: I quote the first and third stanzas of the former and the whole of the latter (from whose title we infer that the writer has lived through, like Camus and others too civilized for the century in which they found themselves, the temptation to suicide). Here in coherent and distanced shape are the contraries, the extremes he suffered.

Tiger Christ unsheathed his sword,
Threw it down, became a lamb.
Swift spat upon the species, but
Took two women to his heart.
Samson who was strong as death
Paid his strength to kiss a slut.
Othello that stiff warrior
Was broken by a woman's heart.
Troy burned for a sea-tax, also for
Possession of a charming whore.
What do all examples show?
What must the finished murderer know?
. . . . .
"What have I said?" asked Socrates,
"Affirmed extremes, cried yes and no,
Taken all parts, denied myself,
Praised the caress, extolled the blow,
Soldier and lover quite deranged
Until their motions are exchanged.
- - What do all examples show?
What can any actor know?
The contradiction in every act,
The infinite task of the human heart."

*

Athlete, virtuoso,
Training for happiness,
Bend arm and knee and seek
The body's sharp distress,
For pain is pleasure's cost,
Denial is the route
To speech before the millions

Or personal with the flute.
Driven by love to this,
As knock-kneed Hegel said,
To seek with a sword their peace,
That the child may be taken away
From the hurly-burly and fed.

Ladies and Gentlemen, said
The curious Socrates,
I have asked, what is this life
But a childermass,
As Abraham recognized,
A working with the knife
At animal, maid and stone
Until we have cut it down
All but the soul alone:
Through hate we guard our love,
And its distinction's known.

Such warring distinctions, when they can no longer be separated or controlled, undermine both the poet's claim on life and the poem's autonomy.

There are two related motives for poetry: one as a means of taking possession of experience, the other as an impulse to self-expression. From whatever bias a poet approaches his self-appointed task, he is necessarily expressing *himself*. Entering the realm of conjecture, one may surmise from internal evidence that Schwartz inclined with extraordinary creative innocence toward the latter forms of spontaneous lyrical expression. Yet what he had to express of himself at the same time was the schism, the contradictions of a "veteran of childhood" in obsessive images of fear and guilt. A poem which accomplishes this task with beautiful clarity and objective candor without capitulating to self-pity or sentimentality is "The Ballad of the Children of the Czar" from which I quote the final section:

Now, in another October
Of this tragic star,

I see my second year,
I eat my baked potato.

It is my buttered world,
But, poked by my unlearned hand,

It falls from the highchair down
and I begin to howl.

And I see the ball roll under
The iron gate which is locked.

Sister is screaming, brother is howling, ,
the ball has evaded their will.

Even a bouncing ball
Is uncontrollable,

And is under the garden wall.
I am overtaken by terror

Thinking of my father's fathers,
And of my own will.

The terrors of choice apparently precipitate mental breakdown, one of the signs of which is that language becomes "uncontrollable", or is used to express a private, subconscious and deeply personal system of meanings.

Drawn to poetry as an act of self-effacing divination, as well perhaps as to the sort of work by which a new self could be affirmed, Schwartz was forced always to return to early wounds, to the "seriousness" dictated by the father who figures in a dialogue poem prescribing, "Be guilty of yourself in the full looking glass." So the poet who strove to transcend the bounds of self in poetry as an act of love acknowledging the priority of music was obliged to express matter for which divination and aspiration, or even charity, were not adequate responses. He finds occasionally "In dark accidents the mind's sufficient grace". But not often enough. Both guesswork and free association play a part in his quest for an unforseeable harmony. He is not looking for the *mot juste* that solves a technical or formal problem so much as proposing myths embodying preconscious associations that, in the later work, tragically degenerate into the repetitive verbal patterns of madness. Spontaneity is evidently cherished but also fatal to his kind of consciousness. The "consummation of consciousness" which he tried to describe in a late and embarrassingly flawed poem, "The Kingdom of Poetry", could in fact only take place outside poetry.

The need to express and at the same time to refrain from expression, or to suppress, appear to be active concomitants in the realization of these poems. Indeed, I suspect that a characteristic imbalance in the tension between these polar wishes - - conscious and unconscious - - stands in a causal relation to the definition of the successful poems on the one hand, and to the redundancy that is not true elaboration occurring in the flawed later poems on the other. So long as his condition could be perceived and felt by the poet as alienated, it issued in some of the most compassionate and indispensible lyric poems of our time (surely an era unconducive to poetry, or even reflection). "In the Naked Bed, in Plato's Cave", "The Heavy Bear Who Goes with Me", "Someone Is

Harshly Coughing as Before", "Tired and Unhappy You Think of Houses", "Calmly We Walk Through This April's Day", all speak to us of our own predicament. ("Time is the school in which we learn, / Time is the fire in which we burn.") They are not a minor writer's exercises in narcissism. A brief passage from his "Prothalamion" is as self-appraisal tragic and detached:

"The voice's promise is easy, and hope
Is drunk and wanton, and unwilled;
In time's quicksilver, where our desires grope,
The dream is warped or monstrously fulfilled.
In this sense, listen, listen, and draw near:
Love is inexhaustible and full of fear."
. . . . .
I am the octopus in love with God,
For thus is my desire inconclusible,
Until my mind, deranged in swimming tubes,
Issues its own darkness, clutching seas
- - O God of my perfect ignorance,
Bring the New Year to my sister soon,
Take from me strength and power to bless her head,
Give her the magnitude of secular trust,
Until she turns to me in troubled sleep,
Seeing me in my wish, free from self-wrongs.

But self-wrongs are precisely the ones we are least prepared to escape. When alienation had progressed to a point beyond return, the verse produced in this state fails to confer order upon the affective experience, but rather reveals that dessication of feeling characteristic of mental illness. The compulsive, purely auditory verbalising and the very proliferation of exclamation points indicate the absence of feeling, the pathetic effort to induce emotion that is unavailable to the disturbed psyche. From "Vivaldi":

O clear soprano like the morning peal of the bluebells,

O the watercolours of the early morning,
con amore and *vivace*! dancing, prancing galloping,
rollicking!
This is the surrender to the splendor of being's becoming and being!

Schwartz was from the first willing to take Shelleyan risks - - both with abstraction and with feeling. He was certainly more entitled to take them, being, one judges, better instructed in both. What he lacked, finally, was the instinct for survival that made his best work possible. As he put it in an ambitious and from more than one point of view impressive narrative poem, "Coriolanus and His Mother: A Dream of Knowledge" (at the end of the fourth act): "Though man walk alone / He steps upon the whole world / and is thrown!"

Perhaps in any such effort, testing as it must contrary resources of consciousness and feeling, failure becomes, as it were, the price of success. Baudelaire, in the second of twenty prose poems translated by Michael Hamburger, "Confiteor of the Artist", expresses a remarkably similar state of mind in similarly exclamatory terms. He concludes: "The study of beauty is a duel in which the artist cries out in terror before being vanquished." I should like to quote a portion of the latter alongside the final lines of Schwartz' "Summer Knowledge".

For summer knowledge is the knowledge of death as birth,
Of death as the soil of all abounding flowering flaring rebirth.
It is the knowledge of the truth of love and the truth of growing:
it is the knowledge before and after knowledge:
For, in a way, summer knowledge is not knowledge at all: it is

> second nature, first nature fulfilled, a new birth
> and a new death for rebirth, soaring and rising out
> of the flames of turning October, burning
> November,
> the towering and falling fires, growing more and
> more vivid and tall
> In the consummation and the annihilation of the blaze
> of fall.

Baudelaire:

How penetrating are the ends of days in autumn! Oh! penetrating to the point of grief! . . . Oh, the vast delight of gazing fixedly, drowning one's glance in the immensity of sky and sea! A little sailing-boat shuddering on the horizon, the paradigin, in its littleness and its isolation, of my irretrievable existence; monotonous melody of the surge; all these things reflect my thoughts, or I reflect theirs (for in the grandeur of reverie the ego is soon lost).

The real terror for Baudelaire, as we know, was boredom, experienced as a kind of annihilation. Yet the moments of exaltation are likewise recorded as a loss of ego. (Schwartz once wrote with whimsical fatalism of "A Dog Named Ego".) The desire for freedom that has been diagnosed as an identifying characteristic of schizophrenia manifests itself clinically as a "loss" of self. It seems as well a classic accompaniment to that contemplation from which poems arise. Poets are lucky to have their art with which to face truth. Moral courage is not always sufficient assistance in supporting the burden of imagination. Leopardi, who has written elsewhere *"ed e rischio di morte il nascimento"*, describes in his poem *"L'infinito"* a strikingly analogous experience:

> . . .
>
> Ma sedendo e mirando, interminati
> spazi di la da quella, e sovrumani

silenzi, e profondissima quiete
io nel pensier mi fingo; ove per poco
il cor non si spaura. E come il vento
odo stormir tra queste piante, io quello
infinito silenzio a questa voce
vo comparando: e mi sovvien l'eterno,
e le morte stagioni, e la presente
e viva, e il suon di lei. Cosi tra quest
immensita s'annega il pensier mio:
e il naufragar m'e dolce in questo mare.

The self-made spaces are interior. The silences so nearly terrifying are virtually products of the attentive consciousness. The seasons themselves represent profound psychic rhythms. The drowning of thought, "this shipwreck", both solicitied and willed, is a sensuous experience. Making metaphor, then, is encompassed in terms equally appropriate to making love.

Feeling qualifies thought to a remarkable degree in so intellectual a poet as Delmore Schwartz. Only in madness does intellectuality drive out feeling, distorting and deadening the verse. The dreams of childhood are not the dreams of reason. In his lifelong preoccupation with his own beginnings, Delmore Schwartz, a tragic example of Freudian man, recognized responsibilities rather than pursued "interpretation": "The infinite task of the human heart." His poems are acts of love and courage that deserve not to be forgotten.

Footnotes
CHAPTER NINE

1. Herbert Marcuse, *Eros and Civilization*, pp. 130 - 131.

Chapter Ten

MRS' WHARTON'S PROFESSION: THE REEF RECONNOITERED

Protected by her great wealth and social position from the austere conditions usually associated with enterprise of any seriousness in the arts, and defended altogether from those abrasive contacts with reality commonly assumed to be indispensable means of deepening and extending the fiction writer's hoard of experience, Edith Wharton - - despite the ready initial circulation her work attained - - has never commanded in her finest productions the audience she deserved. *The Reef*, for example, formally the most interesting, materially the most personal, and emotionally the most complex of her novels is scarcely known, let alone appreciated. Even Edmund Wilson, concerned to do "Justice to Edith Wharton" shortly after her death [1] dismisses *The Reef* parenthetically as a "relapse into 'psychological problems' " - - surely a thoughtless stricture to place upon the work of any writer of fiction. Those who consider that the unabating prose of a lady writer could only function as a vacuous adjunct to her equally unflagging social commitments are on more credible ground, but they too are, as it happens, in this case utterly mistaken.

The Reef is a masterpiece, and a masterpiece that illuminates with unsparing delicacy the predicament of a woman, widowed and with children, a product of the iniquitous sheltering practiced by the upper classes, arriving in her middle years, and by means of the traps her own indoctrinated sensibility sets for her, at a late understanding of her own emotional capacity. Sexuality is not a word that Anna Leath, despite her native intelligence, would have found easy to pronounce. She did not inhabit a world in which penis envy or the female orgasm were staples of conversation. Interestingly enough, the diplomat with whom she falls in love is less the agent of this revelation than a déclassé young girl, Sophy Viner (the governess - - what else?) who has both everything and nothing to lose by her unselfish mediation.

Having been inaccurately "placed" as a literary disciple of her friend Henry James, Mrs. Wharton subsequently had to endure the displeasure of those critics who found her inadequately Jamesean. Hence a further irony attends the unaccountable neglect of this her only work employing the narrative technique perfected by the master in his later phase. He, at least, was appreciative, as a letter dictated from his sickroom at Rye indicates. The beauty of *The Reef* as he sees it lies in its Drama (a word James characteristically capitalizes), and he praises without his customary reservations the "psychologic Racinian unity, intensity and gracility" of the book. Another friend saw in the representation of Anna a "masterly self-diagnosis" of the author, and in that of Anna's fiancé Darrow, her friend of a lifetime Walter Berry "distorted into a prig". Both are undoubtedly right.

Seen in the light of the serious and important work of her middle period, beginning with *Ethan Frome* and *The Reef* in 1911 and 1912 respectively, the profusion of lesser titles during the preceding decade is evidence not of dilettantism but of obsession. The early works subsist rather more as conceptual forms than human transactions. They may indeed be thought to represent the same refuge from intimacy that "society" affords. The old New York of her origins, toward which her writings attest so ambiguous a response, feared ideas as well as assertive emotions. The young Edith Jones, starved for ideas, hungering for an intellectual life, by setting out to overcome these frustrations became a radical non-conformist to her cultural context. Yet in doing so she made a conventional adaptation. Ideas represent not only a safe by a respectable form of excitement; in addition, they represent excellent defenses against less manageable emotions. The words that poured forth so freely from Mrs. Wharton's pen - - all apparently before she emerged from her bedroom promptly at 11:30 each morning - - seem to have served as an impervious defense of her privacy.

Henry James who elaborated the figure of the house of fiction once remarked that whoever would understand "our Edith" must see her in the act of creating a habitation for herself. These dwellings and their gardens, the highly conscious compositions of an impeccable taste with unlimited means to express itself in the variety of The Mount at Lenox, Massachusetts; Le Pavillon Colombe at St-Brice-sous-Forêt; Ste-Claire-le-Chateau in the south of France - - were perhaps formal extensions of those verbal structures (so often equally "impersonal"), the author's sanctuaries from self on the way to accepting the self to be lived with in those environs.

The Reef was composed during what proved to be the most difficult period of Mrs. Wharton's life, a crisis that would undoubtedly have numbed and silenced many another writer, and that ended finally in her divorce. Her husband was, in fact, going insane yet she was unable to persuade his family of the seriousness of his condition. Her friends, who counted themselves also the friends of Teddy, afforded, for the most part by correspondence, only the most qualified consolation. Meanwhile her otherwise mild and amiable husband, a harmless sportsman and engaging host, developed a repertory of irrational rages alternating with interludes of abject dependence equally alarming and evidently incurable.

None of this figures in her memoirs, *A Backward Glance* (1934), a volume more notable for the amount of information it withholds than proffers about the writer's life. The memoirs of tactful friends like Percy Lubbock and even the correspondence are scarcely less concerned with the abridgement of self-revelation, the protection of a privacy to which only her pekinese dogs, her maid, and the enigmatic and unlovably snobbish egoist Walter Berry appeared to enjoy access. For Mrs. Wharton was a social being whose credence in the public rituals of civilized intercourse seems to have amounted to a quasi-sacramental endorsement of their power to establish acceptable distances between individuals rather than to diminish those intervals.

So invincible seems the fortress of privilege and privacy, one finds oneself wondering whether even suffering found its way through to her. Did she ever weep . . . or make love? Or did Anna Leath perform these devoirs for her? The grande dame of photograph and anecdote provides no clue for conjecture. This "conventionally dressed woman, jerky in her movements, somehow ill at ease, with an ugly mouth, shaped like a savings box" (the first impression of Nicky Mariano, Bernard Berenson's secretary and, later, her friend), quite evidently shy but far from timid, appears ordained to authority rather than submission.

"Unexpected obstacle" - - the opening words of The *Reef*, the text of the telegram with which Anna Leath postpones without explanation the arrival at Givré of her fiancé, Darrow, and thus unwittingly provides the occasion to prolong his casual encounter with Sophy Viner in Paris, the cause of all her subsequent tremors of conscience - - these words iterate the theme not only of this book but of virtually everything Mrs. Wharton ever wrote.

These obstacles, generally socially imposed and morally and imaginatively reinforced, tend in *The Reef* to be self-induced, the expression of fears and frustrations fundamental to the author's nature in a way perhaps not hitherto admitted. The Eumenides who dogged the lives of characters in earlier fictions do not here have to be invoked to explain what transpires between Anna Leath, her children, her children's governess and George Darrow. The frivolities that can confer dramatic significance only upon what they destroy, as in the case of Miss Lily Bart in *The House of Mirth*, are not requisitioned as motivating factors in *The Reef* because *The Reef* takes place in a social context which Mrs. Wharton, and we, can take seriously as morally compelling. The traditional social values of France have precisely that stability to recommend them which the raw New World even of Old New York has never known completely - - even while indulging itself in Puritan imitations thereof.

Anna Leath is an example of a transplanted American whose very inexperience assists her in freely accepting the familial duties devoling upon her in respect to her dead husband's French estate and relations. She recalls having been courted by the well-bred Fraser Leath who delighted her with agreeably modulated revolutionary sentiments - - such as the announcement: "Shall you mind, I wonder, if I tell you that you live in a dreadfully conventional atmosphere?" Thus Anna, on the verge of marriage, felt that she had been given "a glimpse of a society at once freer and finer, which observed the traditional forms but had discarded the underlying prejudices; whereas the world she knew had discarded many of the forms and kept almost all the prejudices". And indeed in the well-regulated world of her youth "the unusual was regarded as either immoral or ill-bred, and people with emotions were not visited". Unprepared for strong emotions, though "she had always known that she should not be afraid of them", Anna Leath found no such demands made upon her in her first marriage. Her situation, mutedly analogous to that of Dorothea in *Middlemarch*, is expressed in similar figures: "Life, to Mr. Leath, was like a walk through a carefully classified museum, where, in moments of doubt, one had only to look at the number and refer to one's catalogue; to his wife it was like groping about in a huge dark lumber-room where the exploring ray of curiosity lit up now some shape of breathing beauty and now a mummy's grin." The chateau in which her marriage and widowhood are passed becomes the visible expression both of the narrowing responsibilities to which her nature inclines her and the identity they confer upon her.

> . . . and the house had for a time become to her the very symbol of narrowness and monotony. Then, with the passing of years, it had gradually acquired a less inimical character, had become, not again a castle of dreams, evoker of fair images and romantic legend, but the shell of a life slowly adjusted to its dwelling: the place one came back to, the place where one had one's duties, one's habits and one's books, the place one would naturally live in till one died: a dull house, an inconvenient house, of which one knew all the defects, the shabbiness, the discomforts, but to which one was so used that one could hardly, after so long a time, think one's self away from it without suffering a certain loss of identity. (pp. 84 - 85).

The house at Givré, though it contains her late husband's acquisitions (not least among them being herself), is most obviously not a museum but a habitation. As authoritatively and beautifully realized in its seasonal effects as any impressionist painting, it assumes in its environs nonetheless to George Darrow - - as a figural extension of its mistress - - the magnitude of the obstacle to be converted to his care. While tramping through the woods nearby with the stepson of his hostess, a young man in love with Sophy Viner, Darrow, exerting his diplomatic resources hitherto less strained in his professional role, "had an almost physical sense of struggling for air, of battling helplessly with material obstructions, as though the russet covert through which he trudged were the heart of a maleficent jungle".

A family council, presided over by the Gallic Madame de Chantelle and rendered decisive by the richly comic contributions of Miss Adelaide Painter whose thirty-year residence in Paris has done little to efface the traces of South Braintree, Massachusetts, pronounces in favor of young Owen's suit, Inevitably, this relationship crumbles almost as soon as the cumbersome ceremonies for its ratification are completed. The immature Owen does not bear comparison with Sophy Viner's seducer. Sophy renounced both Owen and Darrow in a gesture that compromises still further her precarious future.

Yet it is on the basis of these renunciations that another of Mrs. Wharton's habitual themes finds paradoxical affirmation. For Anna, devoted in her parental offices, yet caught up in an anguished self-debate that Darrow can do little to alleviate, arrives finally at a sensible apprehension of the futility of sacrifice.

I cannot concur with Blake Nevius [2], on the whole an astute reader of Mrs. Wharton's fiction, in his suggestion that "with Anna Leath the ideal of duty gradually succumbs to her passion for Darrow", A more intelligent and a highly conscious transformation is presented to us: a repertory of precisely registered responses to newly gained emotional knowledge on the part of a mature moral imagination. By a not improbable coincidence, Anna owes her happiness to the same person to whom her son is indebted for his unhappiness. Yet the two are not morally equivalent. Had Sophy Viner elected to accept Owen in marriage neither this acquiescence nor any gesture the mother might perform could within the realm of probability make this youth, at this stage of his development, into either a happy or effective husband. Commonsense and her compassionate tact tell Anna that her best choice in his regard is not to impose herself too insistently. Such is the nature of the relationship of one's sensibility to one's judgment, commonsense and compasionate tact are less easily applied to oneself than to almost any other. Readers in a period like the present when the public consciousness is coming to adapt itself to a new and more equitable appraisal of the role of women, will surely arrive at a more prompt appreciation of the feminist drift of Mrs. Wharton's intentions in portraying Anna. What surely is taking place in Anna's mind is a deepened and enlarged apprehension of the meaning of duty in relation to self-realization.

At the beginning of the novel, Anna was revealed as a sensitive and not unintelligent individual whose circumstances - - however economically protected - - represent a visible constriction of her human possibilities. In common with a long line of female characters both in fiction and out of it, her sensibility and hence her sexual vitality is employed constructively but in a surrogate fashion in aestheticizing what experience her situation permits. By following closely all her hesitations and misgivings on the way to the decision to accept happiness with Darrow, we are permitted, I think, an insight into a process that is the opposite of subjective self-indulgence. Further, we see how costly the abandonment of empty concepts, the culturally induced repressive prospect of a woman's role, can be to the psyche imprinted from childhood with those shallow proprieties.

Readers, - - even the highly "trained" - - tend to respond uncritically to quite gross expressions of bias in those fictional representations that reinforce rather than contradict the culturally accepted stereotypes. Hemingway's transparently prejudiced and crude representations of rebellion, for example, embodied in *The Sun Also Rises* in the arbitrarily masculinized character of Brett, the only complement Hemingway could conceive for Jake's wound, is a case in point. A commensurate tardiness, especially on the part of male readers, in responding to so inner and unfamiliar a drama as Anna's, is only to be expected. Edmund Wilson's patience was tried by *The Reef*, I suppose, on precisely these grounds.

The masculine patience of Darrow within the novel is certainly tried by Anna's suffering, augmented as it is by an active imagination and the delusive supposition that relief will come with documentary evidence of the interlude shared by Darrow with Sophy Viner, an interlude that had little emotional significance for him at the time and virtually none now. His handling of Anna's demand for information she imagines will exorcise her pain is entirely to his credit and indeed restores his integrity as no other choice does in the book.

> "I want to know everything", she repeated. "It's the only way to make me forget."
>
> "No . . . If I did, do you suppose you'd forget that?"
>
> . . . "You see it's impossible", he went on, "I've done a thing I loathe, and to atone for it you ask me to do another. What sort of satisfaction would that give you? It would put something irremediable between us."

Critics have expressed more understandable dissatisfaction with the grotesque final scene in which Anna calls on Sophy's sister in the expectation of seeing Sophy who meanwhile, with selfless prudence and gallantry, has taken herself off, returning to the employment from which she had been escaping when Darrow first encountered her. Yet the vulgarity (all the more shocking in comparison with Anna's civilized domains) of Mrs. McTarvie-Birch and her ambience, evidence of a life messy and confused, is not to be construed as Mrs. Wharton's self-righteous commentary on the absent Sophy's inherent moral inadequacy. The fact that Mrs. McTarvie-Birch is an actress of some kind (". . . As an artist, of course, it's perfectly impossible for me to have her with me . . .") reminds us of Sophy's vulnerable aspirations in the company of Darrow earlier. But the image of grubby transience and the implications of corrupt values seem, rather, an effective projection of the world to which her tragic potential relegates her.

All the participants of a drama may be said to be "actors" and, since life goes on, may be thought to continue acting their elected roles even when we are not watching. So, for that matter, do the very settings in which those roles were determined. While a final image of the chateau, serene in its park, might have been more consoling to the reader, it could not have provided a truer perspective of the cause of Anna's happiness. The hotel from which the unwanted guest has already departed, leaving no fixed address, is a more appropriate inducement to our understanding. With an instinct resembling James' technical assurance, and for the same reasons that led him to withhold the point of view from Charlotte Stant in *The Golden Bowl* to so great an extent, Mrs. Wharton spares us Sophy's sacrificial presence in favour of her predictable fate.

Chapter Ten
FOOTNOTES

1. His essay appears in *The Wound And The Bow* (New York, 1941).

2. *Mrs. Wharton: A Study of Her Fiction* (New York, 1961).

Chapter Eleven

EÇA DE QUEIROZ: THE ARBITRATION OF IRONY

What we look to the great masters for in the way of fiction, Eça has achieved - - not once but repeatedly - - and virtually without acclaim outside his own country. If after some eighty years of obscurity such exceedingly able translations as that of *The Maias* by Patricia McGowan Pinheiro and Ann Stevens should emerge only to be remaindered in Britain, Canada and Australia (while the reading public presumably meditates upon such prose as the Watergate Tapes afford) these are circumstances that Eça, a diplomat by profession and ironist by habitual inclination, would be better qualified than most to appreciate.

The Sin of Father Amaro, (1880), *Cousin Bazilio* (1878), *The Relic* (1887), *The Maias* (1888), to cite only the most obvious instances, if not the work of an inventor in the Poundian sense of the term ("Men who found a new process, or whose extant work gives us the first known example of a process") are most certainly the work of a master "who combined a number of such processes, and who used them as well as or better than the inventors."[1] While the inventors we might call to mind appear almost axiomatically driven to their inventions by their disturbed or ambivalent relations with their material - - for example, the astigmatism attributed to El Greco, the neurosis inherent in the very syntax of the ferociously anti-bourgeois bourgeois Flaubert - - perhaps a very condition of the mastery to which we pay tribute in Eça is the emotional distance he characteristically maintains in adopting the symbolic naturalist's strategy of the effaced narrator. However rigorously the physical Flaubert absents himself from the scene of his fiction, the more forcefully the trained reader feels himself the subect of indoctrination in the nihilism of this author Zola termed the "greatest negator" of a nation whose rational posture communicates a tonic scepticism to most areas of expression. Indeed, whether in *Madame Bovary* or *Bouvard et Pecuchet*, one feels oneself even more drastically a participant in the author's symbolic self-surgery. Obviously, between writers and their subjects, there exist distances and distances the calibration of which necessarily involves evidence both repressed and speculative. Eça, it must be acknowledged, makes a very Tolstoyan Flaubert. Yet there is in Eça's stance *vis-a-vis* his subjects something very "French", due not merely to the accident that the tactics he absorbed were the invention of Frenchmen, but perhaps to a more consciously adopted manner, convincing to the extent that it is "put on" - - like the Britishness of T.S. Eliot. Eça served for some time as the Portuguese Consul in Paris where he died in 1900 at the age of 57. Photographs of the period show him in Mandarin costume in the domestic setting of his garden at Neuilly with a pretty young wife and constrained assortment of children, the apparent recipients of a French upbringing. He bears a rather striking resemblance to Proust.

* * *

Adrian Stokes in an essay on the nature of art has said: "Art wins for connective activity a grain of the finality of death." And further: "Fine building exemplifies the reparative function of art."[2] (Reading and re-reading the works of Eça a number of times over the past several years, always with an undiminished sense of the restorative powers of realism aptly applied, has reinforced my intuition of the applicableness of these notions to the fictions of an artist of Eça's order. Architecture of course is an analogy far from foreign to our concept of the novel. Even the very first novel of Eça, *The Sin of Father Amaro*, represents "fine building" unerringly sustained. In this respect he manages consistently to outshine his models. To those occasions where Flaubert tends to appear contrived or arbitrarily mechanical, or Stendhal casual and impatient with the restrictions of art, Eça brings an unstudied and impartially vital tenor of life.

The Maias in particular impresses me as a compassionate premonitory reparative gesture, a sort of gloss, more satisfying than life *because* it is art, on the moral collapse subsequently enacted in Europe on a scale too enormous for the imagination to encompass. Let it be said that *The Maias* is not another *Magic Mountain*. Although its mode is satire, its method is neither cruel nor doctrinaire, a contingency of that distancing already mentioned. The story relates the downfall of a great family reduced to a single heir, Carlos Eduardo da Maia, by the defection of a frivolous mother, the suicide of an unstable father. Raised by his grandfather Alfonso (one of the secular saints of European literature) along English lines - - the latter as a liberal exile in Richmond having acquired a lasting admiration for things British, reinforced by an equally lasting distaste for clerical interference - - Carlos comes of age: noble, cultivated, idealistic, wealthy, an individual, in short, almost too promising for the context of decadence in which he finds himself in the Lisbon of the late nineteenth century.

Although critics tend to emphasize the romantic burden of compromised heredity, manic depression, passion and incest, Carlos in fact has a high threshold of resistance to the irrational, is never afflicted with his father's nervosity (thanks doubtless to his grandfather's allegiance to the athletic English education) and indeed questions (like Stendhal's young Fabrizio) his own capacity for the total commitment exacted by romantic standards. The incest into which he falls more than halfway through the book is seen to be an utterly plausible occurence. Poignant as are the vicissitudes of this relationship, the fact of its overlapping with an equally fortuitous though altogether more casual affair with Madame Gouvarinho, and the extent to which the anticlimactic survival of its termination on the part of both parties is documented furnishes an oblique criticism of the very notion of "romance". The tragedy of the book is not the tragedy that readers of *Wuthering Heights* prefer to find. It is a tragedy of dilettantism. Which makes this a very modern book.

There is every indication that Eça set out quite consciously to adopt the categories of Balzac and Perez-Galdos by submitting them to the deflationary ironic treatment that became his signature. *The Sin of Father Amaro*, an unsparing picture of clerical corruption, is subtitled in the original: *Scenas da vida devota. Cousin Bazilio* sums up adultery followed by blackmail as: *episodio domestico*. And *The Maias* becomes, inevitably, *Episodios da vida romantica,* a major tactic of which consists in the multiplication of mutually parodistic romantic parallels.

The Maias opens with the transformation of Ramalhete, the long uninhabited family town house in Lisbon, by an interior decorator fetched by Carlos from London, "Jones Bule" to the steward Vilaça who has drawn up a list of the inconveniences of the place. Carlos visits Lisbon often to contribute his aesthetic touches to the year-long operation. Thereafter the book is punctuated at significant intervals by similar interventions of taste, the *mise en scène* for enterprises that never quite get off the ground: the outfitting of a warehouse suitable for Carlos' rarely visited scientific laboratory; consulting rooms for his leisurely medical practice in the Rossio; later, the purchase of his English friend Craft's country house and assembled antiquities in Olivais for Maria. The seriousness of Carlos' intentions or the probability of his achieving notable success at any venture he chooses is not in doubt. We merely become habituated, as he himself does, to the aesthetic procedures with which his temperament and national inclination endow those delays that diffuse his purpose.

A comic analogue of these good intentions is represented by Carlos' good friend Joao da Ega whose unwritten and ever more complex prose epic entitled *Memoirs of an Atom* was already famous among their contemporaries at Coimbra. An ironic foreshadowing of this non-career is provided in chapter four when Alfonso defends his grandson's choice of medicine to the ladies at Santa Olavia who lament that "a boy who was growing up so handsome, such a gentleman, should waste his life prescribing plasters and soiling his hands with blood-letting." To the Judge who wondered if Carlos wanted to be a "real doctor" Alfonso remarks "and why should he not take medicine seriously? If he chooses a profession it is in order that he may follow it with sincerity and ambition like everybody else. I'm not educating him to be a vagabond, much less a dilettante; I'm educating him to be of service to his country." The reader sees him already as both vagabond, an unlikely candidate for resuscitation, morally, politically or culturally.

Eça is especially adept at revealing the ways in which serious discussion among his countrymen tends to degenerate into enthusiastic fantasy. One remarkable scene of this sort is surely modelled on the famous country fair scene in *Madame Bovary* between Emma and Rodolphe, yet the effects are to my mind more complex, the ironies more subtle. Ega is giving a dinner at the Hotel Central in honour of the Banker, Cohen, whom he is concurrently cuckolding. (One of the courses he had thought of was *tomates farcies à la Cohen.*) Talk ranges from the murder of a *fado* singer to the topic of naturalism (for the practice of which Eça has obviously come in for much criticism in Portugal) to the inevitability of bankruptcy and the likelihood of a Spanish invasion. A drunken punch-up is narrowly averted when the topic drifts to modern poetry, ecstatic agreement spontaneously achieved over the matter of how best to resist Galician occupation. Craft volunteers his collection of sixteenth-century swords. And as for Generals? "These could be hired! For example, there was MacMahon! He must be going cheap." Nothing, they decide, regenerates a nation like a terrible drubbing. A bureaucratic observation of the banker's ellicits the overstated and insincere endorsement of the dandy. "Everyone courteously admired Cohen's finesse. He thanked them with a look of emotion as he caressed his whiskers with a hand on which a diamond gleamed. And at that instant the waiters presented a dish of peas in white sauce murmuring: 'Petit pois à la Cohen.' " Less crudely insistent than the interpretation in Flaubert of the prize-giving announcements ("for the best manure" etc.) that serve as a running commentary on the substance of Rodolph's protestations, the ritual presentation of the courses thoughout Ega's dinner has the related function of satire in reducing to scale the substance of the ebb and flow, frequently passionate, not to say *indigeste*, of ideas round the table. The detached presence of the British Craft works in the same fashion, for while his Latin friends are threatening to assassinate each other over a minor poet's "Death of Satan", he sits impassively sipping his chartreuse, mindful that he had frequently had occasion to witness rival schools of literature assailing one another, howling imprecations, knowing that when things had reached this stage a reconciliation with warm embraces was not far off. The dinner ends merrily, ardent toasts being exchanged. And thus the banker finds himself drinking to the Revolution and to Anarchy long before these items became a serious part of the European agenda. The whole is put together like a Rolex watch and quotation to be adequate would exceed the amount space permits. The only comparably extended feasts of social analysis in fiction are, I think, to be found in Tolstoy and Proust.

Literature, for the storyteller, says Georges Piroué, is both an extension of his own existence, and his revenge upon it. Eça's commitment to the tenets of naturalism causes him to share in some respect the pessimism of Flaubert, the pessimism of Proust without however becoming infected either with the former's destructive rage or with the latter's homosexual sense of dispossession from reality. Ortega y Gasset has quite rightly described Proust as "the inventory of a new distance between ourself and things." Eça deserves characterisation as the mediator of a renewable appreciation for the necessary distances between ourselves and things. Since he is not fundamentally compromised by equivocal relations with the objects of his satire (as Proust, for example, by his snobbery), he is able to extract more fun out of them. His books are unusually rich in vignettes that surpass mere caricature, in full scale satiric portraits that fail to infringe upon the humanity of their all-too-credible subjects. A career in the diplomatic service must have provided superior opportunities for observing these specimens.

Among the most amusing of these is the minor figure of Steinbroken, the Finnish Consul, whose diplomatic resources are limited to variations of the phrase *"Voila, c'est très grave"* but who is generally appreciated for his baritone renditions of his native songs "amid which, scattered like pebbles, sounded those bits of words so dear to the Marquis: *frisk, slecht, clikst, glukst."* When the government falls, seemingly from sheer inanition, Steinbroken "in the presence of these political topics, softly withdrew into the window recess and began to wipe his glasses, impenetrable, observing most carefully the neutrality of which Finland was so proud." Ega with irresponsible accuracy asserts: "And so we have the outrageously comic result that the country, which by unanimous consent is the most incompetently governed in all Europe, is bursting with talent! I suggest the following: seeing that the talented men are never any good, let's try the imbeciles for a change!" Addressing the nearest imbecile at hand, he suggests that the Count de Gouvarinho with his geographical interests would make an original Minister of the Navy . . .

> The Count's face shone with pleasure:
> 'Yes, I might consider that . . . But I
> tell you this, my dear Ega, all the
> really fine things, all the great things
> have already been done. The slaves have
> been freed, and taught all they need to
> know of Christianity; they've got custom-
> houses there now . . . It's all been done,
> you see. However, there are still a few
> interesting details to see to . . . Luanda,
> for example, mind - - the final touch that
> progress gives. Luanda, for example, needs
> a theatre, as a civilizing element.'

A day at the races, a charity performance, a scandal and averted duel, the public catalysts of private events, all are rendered with the impressionist's faculty for endowing objective data with subjective signification. Even as the shy and gifted pianist, Cruges, undertakes the thankless task of playing Beethoven's Pathetique sonata to a heedless charity audience (the title, passed along, becomes Sonata Pateta, Fool's Sonata) the elderly democrat senhor Guimaraes, friend of Gambetta, prepares to hand over the untimely information of Carlos' real relationship to Maria, wrapped in an old number of the *Rappel*. The dissolution of Carlos and Maria's idyll, already parodied in Ega's rendezvous with Rachel Cohen amid the grim splendors of the Villa Balzac, the detritus of empty champagne bottles, cold lunches, discarded hairpins, is grotesquely foreshadowed in Ega's traumatic ejection - - costumed as Mephistopheles - - from the Cohen's masked ball. Yet the transmission of the painful truth of his incest to Carlos by the steward Vilaça is irrevocably associated with the latter's search for his misplaced hat.

Few can have mastered the art of anticlimax as has Eça. The final pages of each of his novels leave us with images both hopeless and hopeful of continuing life, of the incapacity of one to appreciate the tragedy he instigates, the incapacity of another to surrender to his own perception of the grounds for disillusion. After the death of Luiza (Eça's Portuguese Emma Bovary) in *Cousin Bazilio*, the unscathed seducer is seen leaping jauntily from a cab and saluting a friend:

> 'Do you know what's happened?' he asked.
> 'No! Do tell me!'
> 'Well, my cousin has just died.'
> 'Poor dear!' murmured Raynaldo, politely.
> They walked down the street together, arm in arm. It was a lovely day, cold, yet frisky with Atlantic ozone. While they walked, Bazilio spoke of Luiza. The delicate viscount lamented that the poor lady had had to die in such nice weather. But nevertheless he thought such relationships absurd.
> He said he did not want to speak ill of the dead. But after all, Bazilio himself had told him that she wore cotton stockings. What horror! It was obvious that she lacked 'style'. She was just a dolled-up sack - - so why worry?
>
> Yes, but just for those couple of months I was here . . .' said Bazilio with his head bowed.
> 'Yes! Yes! Just as a measure of hygiene,' said Raynaldo, condescendingly.
> They walked on in silence. Then they began to laugh at a man who was ineptly driving two black horses in a phaeton. Only in Lisbon could you see such rotten style!
>
> When they got back from their walk, Raynaldo said,

caressing his side whiskers. 'So it appears, for the time being, you're a widower.'

Bazilio smiled resignedly. Then striking the pavement furiously with his walking stick, he exclaimed, 'What a bloody idiot I was! I could have brought Alphonsina along with me anyway!'

Then they both went to have a sherry at the English Tavern.

(trans. by Roy Campbell)

In another street scene *The Maias* ends with Carlos returning from his vagabondage of some years with the news of Maria's marriage in France to encounter his old friend Ega. They agree philosophically upon the uselessness of effort in this world. Ega follows:

'If I was told that a Rothschild fortune or the imperial crown of Charles V awaited me down the road here if I ran, I wouldn't quicken my pace! . . . And both of them slowed down as they walked down the Santos Ramp, as if that were the path of life, at whose end they were sure to find dust and disillusion, along which they should therefore advance with due deliberation and disdain. They could see the Aterro and its long row of lamps. Suddenly Carlos stopped with a gesture of annoyance. 'Confound it! I've come all the way from Paris as hungry as a hunter and I've forgotten to order a dish of Parma ham and peas for the dinner tonight.'

Ega spies a tram which they can catch if they hurry. They set off briskly and are, when last seen, running desparately down the hill and along the Aterro after the elusive red light of the tram. Thus Eça out-Chekhovs Chekhov. No fluid pudding, this, but a panorama of human behaviour so distinctive in its diversity as to defy mere summary, mere analysis.

Chapter Eleven
FOOTNOTES

1. Ezra Pound, *A.B.C. of Reading.*

2. *The Image in Form, Selected Writings,* p. 68.

3. *Proust's Way* (London, 1957).

Chapter Twelve

NABOKOV'S ADA: WORD'S END

Nabokov's ADA is a supremely literary product of quite distinctly limited literary virtue. If this book is to be enjoyed, it must be enjoyed as a piece of confectionary archeology, as a joke on the novel (and on the expectations of certain kinds of readers) rather than Litra-chore, as his heroine might put it. If anyone in our lamentable century is equipped to fulfill Flaubert's expressed wish of writing a novel "about nothing", surely it is Nabokov who with ADA has succeeded in perpetrating a feat of style (or, more properly, a feat of styles) to the virtual exclusion of substance, to the extent of 598 pages, in a language not his own. This is not to suggest that Nabokov is an engineer of prose, he is of course a connoisseur of prose; this is his gift and yet the gift is responsible in some respect for his deficiencies as a novelist. There is no substitute for intelligence. And intelligence is what one most responds to in Nabokov's work. Yet neither is there in the art of the novel an easy substitute for that consciousness, that self-effacing absorption in human behaviour from which the motives for fiction characteristically derive. The convention of fiction is to be about people. Nabokov's fictions are about people only in the most negligently fabricated sense. He is interested in the behaviour of language, not people, and - - after language - - in the thingyness of things. A remark in his little book on Gogol to the effect that "his work, as all great literary achievements, is a phenomenon of language and not one of ideas"[1] has obvious relevance to Nabokov's own work, and never more obviously than in ADA. The consciousness of the scrabble addict, the crossword puzzle composer, the butterfly collector, the aristocrat created ADA and has constructed therein a diversion, a leisurely word game, but nothing so irreducibly vulgar, so tenaciously middle class as a novel. For the kinds of recognitions toward which fiction tends, a writer of Nabokov's sensibility prefers to distance, to transfer to things by means of description. He does not dramatize. He does not readily or convincingly relinquish point of view to his characters. Like a highly skilled fugitive who desires nevertheless to be caught, he proliferates clues rather than presents an action. The aloofness of the exile, the self-absorption of the displaced person are both relieved and relived and ultimately reinforced in public fantasies that solicit readers with a kind of contempt.

The private language of happy families with which ADA is replete is as naturally a mode of exclusion as it is a mode of inclusion. The reader is invited to detect; he can never become a sharer. The vanity and trivial-mindedness of the Veens, along with the concessions toward "plot" in ADA, are as much a way of putting the reader in his place as of satisfying the demands of solipsism. The humility that does not figure in Nabokov's relations with his craft or with his readers occurs only, and I think not insignificantly, in his own autobiography SPEAK, MEMORY. One can achieve suitable deference toward that which one's deepest experience affirms is truly there.

Nabokov's art is an art of violated expectations: his and ours. His tactics are uniquely parodistic. If irony is defensive, a reaction of the cheated, the disillusioned, representing an am--biguous response, it is deomonstrably a technique of discovery in literature. Parody is perhaps a more extreme reaction to similar deprivation, but it is the response of the made-up mind. According to Thomas Mann, a writer for whom Nabokov has little reverence, "the love for a form of art, in the historical possibility of which one can believe no more, will inevitably beget parody".[2] Not simply the "form" of the novel but the antecedent forms of life are for Nabokov no longer commodities inducing rational belief. The rich, humanly availing and secure world of Nabokov's childhood and youth, disposed of by history, consigned to memory, furnishes the local details less for a criticism of life than toward the discrediting of the very tradition of symbolic realism in the novel. A garbled throwaway version of Tolstoy's opening sentence in *Anna Karenina* begins *Ada or Ardor: A Family Chronicle* - - and its pertinence is immediately disclaimed.

We are repeatedly warned by such tricks that the ensuing narrative neither aims to assuage nostalgia nor to induce it (though one suspects that a large measure of Nabokov's fun is derived precisely from confecting those ingredients that will satisfy the corrupted tastes and stock responses of the best-seller's audience even while mocking them).

The Veen family, with the possible exception of Van's mother, Aqua, are not an attractive lot. A less parodistic representation would doubtless have rendered them insupportable to all but the most fascinated students. The suicide of Aqua, wittily accomplished in the pastoral setting of the luxurious looney bin in the likes of which she had passed the better part of her incomparably lucid life, latterly under the care of a Doctor Sig Heiler, "whom everyone venerated as a great guy and near-genius in the usual sense of near-beer", affords Nabokov his usual anti-Freudian set piece. On the other hand, we learn that the notion she is Van's mother may likewise be an hallucination of her madness. As the ants queue to get at her "pretty pills", she signs her suicide note: "My sister's sister who *teper' iz ada* ('now is out of hell')." The sister in question, Marina, a faded actress, presides unobservantly over the Anti-terrestrial paradise at Ardis Hall where her daughters Ada and Lucette together fall inextricably in love with their cousin, Van, at this time a schoolboy of fourteen. Ada, the elder sister, at twelve enjoys the consolations of reciprocated passion. The vigorous erotic life thus begun, interrupted for various lengthy interludes during their educations and her marriage (to an Arizonian cattle rancher of distinguished lineage), culminates in a happily shared senectitude devoted largely to the pursuit of butterflies in remote places subsequent to the suicide of Lucette and the appropriate deaths of husband and uncles. (Lucette, like Aqua, takes pills, reinforcing their effect with doses of alcohol and a plunge from the deck of the luxury liner on which Van, too, was travelling to Manhattan. Daniel Veen, an art dealer and presumably an echo of the famous Duveen, never really cared much for painting; he perishes haunted by the fakes of Hieronymous Bosch from which he had gained a fortune. His brother "Demon" Veen, Van's father, departs more conventionally in a spectacular air crash over the Pacific.)

Beyond the lyricized opulence of setting and atmosphere, one can scarcely fail to sense that the real topic, the burden of meaning implicit in the lovers' preposterous idyll lies not in their much exercised *amour* or its circumambient literary glosses - - not the flourishing passion of the 97-year old memoirist and his collaboratrix but its persistent isolationism. Not their joyous sensuality but their heartlessness distinguishes this pair. The superior ration of intelligence their creator has donated to them reveals more incisively their repellent selfishness. Ada's name does signify in Russian "hell" as well as sexual ardor. Without perceptible compunction she acknowledges to Van ". . . we *teased* her to death. . . . . . . And indeed Lucette's drowning may convince us that death rather than life-sustaining love is what this book is about. Death and ontological solitude.

These themes recur consistently in a variety of forms through such earlier works as *Invitation to a Beheading* (1935),

The Real Life of Sebastian Knight (1941), and *Bend Sinister* (1946). They reappear in *Ada* in a fantasied context, the anachronistic amalgam of the author's homeland with all the countries of his prolonged exile. The elaborated verbal games, the irrational excursions, the invented grotesqueries of this monstrous fairy tale partially mask but never wholly conceal this fundamental preoccupation with isolation, loss, exile, rejection, and death - - not as ideas but as experience.

Lucette's death is described from several points of view by the promiscuously omniscient narrator. Her last moments of consciousness are subjectively rendered:

> As she began losing track of herself, she thought it proper to inform a series of receding Lucettes - - telling them to pass it on and on in a trick-crystal regression - - that what death amounted to was only a more complete assortment of the infinite fractions of solitude. (p. 494)

The infinite fractions of the writer's solitude have made him a specialist in consciousness. If Nabokov has no interest in observing any set of conventions devised in the Jamesian manner to preserve the probabilities of naturalistic fiction, neither is he impelled by any overriding argumentative bias to tyrannize over his human materials as, for example, does D.H. Lawrence. Not conceptual forms but the immediacy of mental experience engages his preemptive attention as an artist. This most intelligent of writers does not write philosophical novels. He shares with Proust the realization that *all* experience is mental experience, that our consciousness is our only means of possessing impressions, and memory and imagination of retaining them.

Time fascinates Nabokov sufficiently for him to have provided his character Van with an undeserved professorship so that an essay on the texture of time could be included in *Ada*. (Van chooses to deliver his lectures by means of a voice recorder kept in his pocket, though presenting himself in person and moving his lips. When the recorder fails on one occasion, he prefers to feign a heart attack and be carried out rather than to attempt to sort out his notes *ex tempore*.) The point to be made is that even here the focus is not upon an abstract idea but upon a perceived, a felt phenomenon: the texture of time as it impinges upon consciousness. Van's treatise is prefigured interestingly by remarks in the first chapter of Nabokov's autobiography describing how at first he "groped for some secret outlet only to discover that the prison of time is spherical and without exits. . ." (p. 20), then, how - - still as a child:

> I felt myself plunged abruptly into a radiant and mobile medium that was none other than the pure element of time. One shared it - - just as excited bathers share shining sea-water - - with creatures that were not oneself but that were joined to one by time's common flow, an environment quite different from the spatial world, which not only man but apes and butterflies can perceive. (*Speak, Memory*, pp. 21-22)

Perhaps these states of intensified awareness do not differ qualitatively from Wordsworth's "spots of time", yet we can be grateful that Nabokov, while being an amazingly productive writer, has never shown the slightest indication of becoming a romantic one.

The rich precision, the concentrated exactness of Nabokov's observation, seemingly the product of the acutely heightened awareness of the insomniac, remain among his strongest assets. These qualities are perhaps also a symptom of his alienation from the new world that circumstances compelled him to call his own. It is useless but nevertheless interesting to speculate on the development Nabokov's talents might have undergone had he never left Europe. To adopt a new language and a new country as unaccommodating to the non-commercial arts as America could fail to be self-defeating, one conjectures, only for a writer of journalism . . . or a formidable wit. For, since the Boston Tea Party, has American culture transformed itself into an experience that a foreigner can take seriously? One presumes that out of fascinated horror Nabokov became a collector and cataloguer of jargon and vulgarisms, an authority on motels, a stylish mimic of the styleless, a comic expositor of adolescent sexuality. His sustained flirtation with the irrational (perfected in *Pale Fire*) may be the saving aspect of temperament and, at the same time, without doubt the response best calculated to see one through a professorial assignment in the American academe. A not altogether unkindly disposed fate has arranged with suitable irony that Nabokov's most receptive readers should be numbered among those towards whom, collectively, his condescension is a kind of armament.

The country maliciously described as having passed from barbarism to decadence without knowing civilization has been served better than it deserves by Nabokov's cultural embassy. *Ada* is a formidable book, though readers will have to be forgiven for finding it formidable chiefly in being unwieldy to hold. Its dionysian pedantry makes it the most sustained act of frivolity in modern literature. The manic flights of inconsequence from which its story draws life become in their extravagance the book's main claim to consequence, for by means of this organized madness Nabokov has pretty well left nothing undissected that has to do with romantic feeling, romantic attitudes, and the romantic poses upon which literature has so long been parasitic. This is a book so marvelously subversive that its very targets will remain ignorant of their exposure. Yet if it questions the assumptions upon which bourgeois literature has flourished, it also brings us unbearably close to a precipice that no writer approaches without fear either in dreams or awake: the void that opens between his own words and the reality they imitate. To give to words an independent "reality", to perceive language as color, are refuges that Nabokov has taken but in which he is not comfortable either. A "teasy problem" demanded Dr. Veen's presence back at the clinic (on p. 468): "a singular case of chromesthesia" afflicting one Spencer Muldoon, "born eyeless, aged forty, single, friendless . . . known to hallucinate during fits of violent paranoia, calling out the names of such shapes and substances as he had learned to identify by touch, or thought he recognized through the awfulness of stories about them (falling trees, extinct saurians) and which now pressed on him from all sides . . ." The teasy problem is one of Nabokov's little jokes at the expense of the scientific pretensions of psychology. But Muldoon's "iridian recall", his account of the "gamut of 'stingles' " by which he feels color is, I would guess, with comic amplification a fairly truthful transcript of the author's alert and sleepless mind assailed by language. The mad chess master's obsession in *The Defense* is another, and to my mind, more compelling variation on this theme.

The "much, much more" to which the writer archly refers at the end of his parodistic summary of the content of his book *is* words - - so arranged that when we have got what fun there is to be had from the charades we can begin to fear intelligently the senseless void words tend against.

Chapter Twelve
FOOTNOTES

1. *Editions Poetry* (London, 1947) p. 151.

2. I quote from Erich Heller's *Thomas Mann, The Ironic German*, (New York, 1961) p. 253.

Chapter Thirteen

HYSTERIA NATURALIZED

Reading - - this most seductive of pilgrmages, "a structuring activity" as the editors of *Tel Quel* would have it - - was enbarked upon by me in Danville, Illinois while the Spanish Civil War raged blocks away at the Bijou or Orpheum. After so many heuristic excursions to so many libraries, the vocation to criticism is somehow associated in my mind with the election of Roosevelt. My father's representations of the catastrophic consequences certain to ensue (a notion evidently shared by most of the citizens of Danville, judging from the drifts of Landon buttons by the curbside when the voting was over) were so convincing that I remember spending some time in a state of exalted apprehension listening and watching from our second storey window for the Nazi Storm Troops to turn the corner into our quiet street - - hours that, admittedly, might better have been spent with the Bobs Hill Boys on safari through any vacant lot. This revelation of the fallibility of grownups marks the probable beginning of my vocation to doubt.

Now, many cataclysms later, in good faith (though not without profound misgivings) I set aside my New Critical artillery (American style) in order to respond to the invitation of the Nouvelle Critique (Barthesian version) which prescribes that one place one's "deepest self", this bookworm, at the disposal of the text so that a dialogue between our several historical situations and subjectivities may occur.

Although Monsieur Barthes has urged us to think of literature as the "Utopia of language" (in *Writing Degree Zero*) he assures the reader (in his essay "What is Criticism") that "the critic is not responsible for reconstructing the work's message but only its system." He nevertheless advises us to think of criticism as "no more than a language (or, more precisely, a metalanguage)" since only thus can criticism be "paradoxically but authentically - - both objective and subjective, historical and existential, totalitarian and liberal." Yet, having chosen a langauge (his metaphor for system') the critic, he tells us, has in fact chosen a *necessity* (Barthes' italics) "the end product of a certain historical ripening", yet an exercise in which he puts "all his 'profundity', i.e., his choices, his pleasures, his resistances, his obsessions. Thus begins at the heart of the critical work, the dialogue of two histories and two subjectivities, the author's and the critic's."[1]

Such impressionistic formulations, unencumbered with a scholar's gestures toward substantiation, seem to exert an irresistible attraction upon the undergraduate mind, at least in Paris where the master practices. The invitation to subversiveness is all the more appreciable in France where the young are subjected to a more persistently authoritarian upbringing than elsewhere. The restricted literacy of the North American student renders all but the most sophisticated graduate students immune to the structuralist invitation. Yet it does not take much perspicacity to see a criticism so conceived attaining equal status with and eventually superseding literature. Thus, for the sake of the dialogue, I must confess that my own reaction began in exasperation and tapered off into something resembling despair - - until I came to realize that this is what the exaggerated vanity, the rococo rhetoric, the feverish modernism signify: the failure of affect, nihilism, the refusal of memory (a cultural reflex in France whose history since the Fourth Republic has been so incompatible with the myth of superiority purveyed in the schools). Perhaps, as a French writer Yves Velan so quaintly expresses it, "Perhaps these books are merely the successive moments of a pure itinerary."[2] The very profusion and inconsistency of Barthes' prodigious bibliography of the past few years suggests that it can only emanate from hysteria.

Although "crisis" is a word that must be uttered more often in France than "mother", the commotion created by structuralism seems to me no more profound than that of any other fashion succeeding an outmoded predecessor. The French are, in truth, easily bored. Dogmatists at heart but lacking the capacity for sustained attention, they make up in intensity what is wanting in depth. Roland Barthes, like many another Frenchman, from shopkeepers to the faculty of the Hautes Etudes, is essentially an anarchist courting a system. To look for development or consistency in the works of Barthes would be pointless, but to scrutinize the rituals he invokes might be of some passing interest.

And if my own resistances, pleasures and obsessions herein revealed derive preeminently from my capacity as reader, Barthes' generation and mine is perhaps the last that can make this statement, which will be construed - - if indeed it is even noticed - - as a confession of inadequacy by a generation to whome imperviousness to the mediating function of the word has become the cultural norm.

Making oneself as disponible as possible to the multitudinous texts of Barthes, his jannisaries and detractors (no mean task at this stage of his prolific career), reading or, rather, "decoding" and "naturalizing" as the saying goes, one recognizes in them all the signs of a hyper-verbal culture in decay (a culture so pervasively verbal that the survival of any French schoolboy in the estimation of his peers is more likely to entail mastery of the fast comeback than exhibitions of strength). What my subjectivity detects in his subjectivity is (not surprisingly) another bookworm, but a worm decidedly "turned" by boredom. And I find interesting confirmation of this diagnosis in Barthes' own admission in the recent *Ecrivains de toujours* volume on himself.[3]

> Enfant, je m'ennuyais souvent et beaucoup. Cela a commencé visiblement très tot, cela s'est continué toute ma vie, par bouffées . . . et cela s'est toujours vu. C'est un ennui panique, allant jusqu'à la détresse: tel celui que j'éprouve dans les colloques, les conférences, les soirées étrangères, les amusements de groupe: partout ou l'ennui PEUT SE VOIR. L'ennui serait-il donc mon hystérie?

The text is illustrated with a two-page spread of photographs documenting accredited moments of kindred distress in the life of the protagonist from childhood to professorship.

Such symptoms are nothing if not learned. They arise, one would judge, not from any pathology of the individual but precisely from the pathology of the cultural context, the context being in a sense that of the romantic period of the nineteenth century: a specifically literary context providing ample inducement to the alert schoolboy (for there is always a time-lag where the educational system is concerned, a time-lag nowhere more pronounced than in France) to apprehend the code, indeed to imitate its procedures. Thus the spleen of Baudelaire and the melancholia of Flaubert linger not merely on the printed page but in the recurrent migraines, the hysteric boredom, the introspective isolationism of the well-indoctrinated pupil who continues to live out the attitudes and emotive postures offered by the printed page - - only to parody them later in the manic "structurations" of his maturity. The adolescent, having only confused intuitions to start with, must learn his emotions from others and his most extreme resistances simply reinforce and call attention to his excessive susceptibility during this universally unhappy time. It happens to bookworms everywhere, but one fancies that in France, in the sanatoria of

Barthes' youth, the milieu proved more conducive to this sort of mimesis than perhaps anywhere else in Europe during the 'forties. The notion at any rate would probably not be offensive to Barthes whose very structuralist proclivities may easily be read as an extension of this habit of mind. (One is tempted to attribute Barthes' myopic historic sense as well to the habitual self-absorption dictated by the romantic code and enforced by the tubercular patient's regime.) Saussure's dated linguistics[4] confer, I suspect, the necessary intimations of form upon an enterprise preconsciously determined in an impressionistic direction.

This impressionism and the rhetorical generalizations endemic to it, exasperating to a less than adulatory audience by reason chiefly of its refusal to maintain itself in a single mode long enough to be convincing, betrays its origins in boredom by willful alterations in the tactical application of its own structures from book to book. Wistfully, one wishes the hysteria had taken a more Flaubertian form, for if the semantic avarice exhibited by a text from Flaubert offers pleasures of definition to the reader that can only have been torment for the writer, Barthes' hysteria, taking the form of verbal incontinence, represents a different response to the pleasure principle. Barthes need not have told us, as he has, "Boredom is not far from ecstacy; it is ecstacy seen from the shores of pleasure."[5] We can see it at work in Barthes' two hundred page "polymorphous meditation" (the words are those of the American translator who should know) on Balzac's twenty-five page effort, the story *Sarrazine*. What are the 561 *lexies* of S/Z and the semantic divagations for which they provide the incitement if not a manic parody of the French schoolboy's perpetual chore, the *explication de texte*? An enterprise all the more piquant, surely, for having been carried out over a two-year period in the seminar rooms of the Ecole Pratique des Hautes Etudes.

The system that disclosed itself to Barthes in Balzac's story (not without the collaterial precedents of Vladimir Propp's *Morphology of the Folktale*, Benveniste's "Semiologie de la langue", and Greimas' functional analyses of dynamic and static predicates) as five "codes": the proairetic (to do with plot), the hermaneutic (to do with suspense and peripateia), the symbolic (signals of themes like raisins in pudding), the referential (internal clues to the cultural context) in fact illuminates nothing that any sophomore needs to lose sleep over. Whatever his critical credentials may be, and he has taken care to announce that he is committed to the search for "validities" in literature rather than "truth", Barthes recognizes a useful pedagogical trick when he comes across one. Clearly, many a harmless hour may be passed in plucking out the codes from the contexts. The stupifying obviousness of the semiological classifications that renders them so suitable for pedagogical purposes severely restricts their utility as instruments of revelation of the conscious artistry of literary work of the first intensity. As imaginative projections, the Saussurian categories offer a more adequate frame of reference for examining the bourgeois myths of everyday life. Thus Barthes adopted their ideological framework for the series of subjective reflections on "*le strip-tease, le tourisme, le biftek et les frites*" and other phenomena of French daily life in *Mythologies*, originally a series of newspaper pieces published on a monthly basis in *Lettres Nouvelles*. Similarly, in *Système de la mode*, he has applied himself to the rhetoric of fashion-as-described (rather than fashion-as-worn) with admittedly flawed results. Even the trivialities of popular culture are too complex in their ramifications to yield their intelligibility readily for inventory by means of a linguistic grid.

The conceptual poverty of a methodology applied with complacent abandon to the texts of Proust as well as the scrutiny of menus and bicycle races has not daunted the practitioners of structuralism. Who could take exception in an enquiry the professed object of which is the retrieval of the structures of internal relations that endow a literary work with its characteristic density and resiliance? One's disappointment at the meagre and confused illumination attributable to the models of intelligibility Barthes extrapolates can be quite easily located. He has himself, in devaluing language, performed his own work of demolition upon his premises. In depicting the writer as the virtually helpless tool of his socially inherited expression (while skillfully exempting himself as critic from vulnerability to the same malady), he borrows, without ideological scruples, a marxist notion, but only, it seems, in order to make literature a more manageable entity: the very tactic Barthes so despises in the historical critics who represent an entrenched establishment to be overthrown.

Although valuation of literature in its content is disavowed by Barthes in favor of testing the "validities" of literary "systems", the annexation of literature as a disenfranchised colony of the social sciences certainly has a punitive aura about it and limits the options of literature to an inventory only marginally more interesting than that of a used car. Like other systems before it, structuralism applied to literature offers the illusion of newness and of a certain objectivity along with the license for total subjectivity. The anthropologist Levi-Strauss himself, who may be though of as having started it all, whose immense undertaking in *Mythologiques*, whose *Tristes Tropiques, La Pensee Sauvage, Le Cru et le cuit* among other beautifully written works retain their rich suggestiveness even for the non-specialist reader, even when their argument provokes doubts, appreciated the dubious and deceptive nature of structural analysis adapted to literature. For primitive myths - - his own central concern - - have no author, a perception that lead Levi-Strauss to postulate the mind itself as the source at its deepest level of those laws governing the creation of myths. The unconscious, in other words, becomes the first structuralist Thus Levi-Strauss expressed his purpose not to show "how men think in myths but how myths think in men without their knowing." ("comment les mythes se pensent dans les hommes, et à leur insu": *Le Cru et le cuit*, p. 20). The language of music, on the other hand, because it is a language without a speaker, he observes, is ideally accessible to the structural treatment linguistics invokes. The problem with literature obviously is that it is never unmediated. In the words of Tzvetan Todorov, the Russian formalist and colleague of Barthes, "Literature enjoys, as we know, a particularly privileged status among semiotic activities. Literature uses language both as a point of departure and as a point of arrival; language endows literature with its abstract configuration as well as its perceptible medium; language is simultaneously mediator and mediated. Consequently literature is not only the first field that can be studied starting from language but also the first field the knowledge of which can cast new light on the properties of language itself."[6]

Having generalized the author adroitly out of existence even before addressing a Johns Hopkins symposium on the topic *"Ecrire: Verbe intransatif?"* Barthes fills the space formerly occupied by the author in relation to the product of his mind with the notions of *ecriture* and *lecture* in conventional tandem: writing as a dehumanized institution and reading as an act of naturalization. That this artful substitution was accomplished not without a certain violence to history did not escape his fellow symposiasts. Professor Paul de Man reproached him with distorting history because he needs a "historical myth of progress to justify a method which is not yet able to justify itself by its results." Only Professor Georges Poulet seems to have noticed that Barthes avoids the use of the word *thought* as if it were obscene. ("On the contrary," counters Barthes, "it is because it is not obscene enough. For me, language is obscene, and that is why I continually return to it.")

Reading and thinking, it is true, are not innocent occupations. Both the one and the other require strategies of accommodation, and language in which to perform it. A Barthesian emphasis on the *signifiant* at the expense of the *signifié*, on form at the expense of content undermines the very condition of literature and renders art beside the point. If criticism is a metaphor for reading, structuralism as purveyed by Barthes is a degree zero of formalism so self-sufficient as to require only token support from the literary object it replaces. The semio-critic, as Barthes would prefer to be called, then becomes an entrepreneur presiding over a steadily diminishing field where the play of relations becomes finally no more than the echo of his own ponderously empty terminology.

"Literature", said Pound in his *ABC of Reading*, "does not exist in a vacuum." Criticism, if it is arrogant enough, apparently can.

Chapter Thirteen
FOOTNOTES

1. "What is Criticism," *Critical Essays* (Evanston, 1972), p.260.

2. Yves Velan, "Barthes," in *Modessy French Criticism*, ed. J. K. Simon (Chicago & London, 1972), p. 311.

3. *Roland Barthes* (Paris, 1975), p. 28.

4. Saussure died in 1913.

5. *Le Plaisure du Texte*, p. 43, my translation.

6. "Language and Literature," in *The Language of Criticism and The Sciences of Man*, pp. 125 - 126.

COSTERUS. Essays in English and American Language and Literature.

Volume 1. Amsterdam 1972. 240 p. Hfl. 40.–
GARLAND CANNON: Sir William Jones's Translation-Interpretation of Sanskrit Literature. SARAH DYCK: The Presence of that Shape: Shelley's *Prometheus Unbound.* MARJORIE ELDER: Hawthorne's *The Marble Faun:* A Gothic Structure. JAMES L. GOLDEN: Adam Smith as a Rhetorical Theorist and Literary Critic. JACK GOODSTEIN: Poetry, Religion and Fact: Matthew Arnold. JAY L. HALIO: Anxiety in *Othello.* JOHN ILLO: Miracle in Milton's Early Verse. F. SAMUEL JANZOW: De Quincey's "Danish Origin of the Lake Country Dialect" Republished. MARTIN L. KORNBLUTH: The Degeneration of Classical Friendship in Elizabethan Drama. VIRGINIA MOSELY: The "Dangerous" Paradox in Joyce's "Eveline". JOHN NIST: Linguistics and the Esthetics of English. SCOTT B. RICE: Smollett's *Travels* and the Genre of Grand Tour Literature. LISBETH J. SACHS and BERNARD H. STERN: The Little Preoedipal Boy in Papa Hemingway and How He Created His Artistry.

Volume 2. Amsterdam 1972. 236 p. Hfl. 40.–
RALPH BEHRENS: Mérimée, Hemingway, and the Bulls. JEANNINE BOHLMEYER: Mythology in Sackville's "Induction" and "Complaint". HAROLD A. BRACK: Needed – a new language for communicating religion. LEONARD FEINBERG: Satire and Humor: In the Orient and in the West. B. GRANGER: The Whim-Whamsical Bachelors in Salmagundi. W. M. FORCE: The What Story? or Who's Who at the Zoo? W. N. KNIGHT: To Enter lists with God. Transformation of Spencerian Chivalric Tradition in Paradise Regained. MARY D. KRAMER: The Roman Catholic Cleric on the Jacobean Stage. BURTON R. POLLIN: The Temperance Movement and Its Friends Look at Poe. SAMUEL J. ROGAL: Two Translations of the Iliad, Book I: Pope and Tickell. J. L. STYAN: The Delicate Balance: Audience Ambivalence in the Comedy of Shakespeare and Chekhov. CLAUDE W. SUMERLIN: Christopher Smart's A Song to David: its influence on Robert Browning. B.W. TEDFORD: A Recipe for Satire and Civilization. H. H. WATTS: Othello and the Issue of Multiplicity. GUY R. WOODALL: Nationalism in the Philadelphia National Gazette and Literary Register: 1820–1836.

Volume 3. Amsterdam 1972. 236 p. Hfl. 40.–
RAYMOND BENOIT: In Dear Detail by Ideal Light: "Ode on a Grecian Urn". E. F. CALLAHAN: Lyric Origins of the Unity of 1 Henry IV. FRASER DREW: John Masefield and Juan Manuel de Rosas. LAURENCE GONZALEZ: Persona Bob: seer and fool. A. HIRT: A Question of Excess: Neo-Classical Adaptations of Greek Tragedy. EDWIN HONIG: Examples of

Poetic Diction in Ben Jonson. ELSIE LEACH: T. S. Eliot and the School of Donne. SEYMOUR REITER: The Structure of 'Waiting for Godot'. DANIEL E. VAN TASSEL: The Search for Manhood in D. H. Lawrence's 'Sons and Lovers'. MARVIN ROSENBERG: Poetry of the Theatre. GUY R. WOODALL: James Russell Lowell's "Works of Jeremy Taylor, D.D.'

Volume 4. Amsterdam 1972. 233 p. Hfl. 40.–
BOGDDY ARIAS: Sailor's Reveries. R. H. BOWERS: Marlowe's 'Dr. Faustus', Tirso's 'El Condenado por Desconfiado', and the Secret Cause. HOWARD O. BROGAN: Satirist Burns and Lord Byron. WELLER EMBLER: Simone Weil and T. S. Eliot. E. ANTHONY JAMES: Defoe's Autobiographical Apologia: Rhetorical Slanting in 'An Appeal to Honour and Justice'. MARY D. KRAMER: The American Wild West Show and "Buffalo Bill" Cody. IRVING MASSEY: Shelley's "Dirge for the Year": The Relation of the Holograph to the First Edition. L. J. MORRISSEY: English Street Theatre: 1655–1708. M. PATRICK: Browning's Dramatic Techniques and 'The Ring and the Book': A Study in Mechanic and Organic Unity. VINCENT F. PETRONELLA: Shakespeare's 'Henry V' and the Second Tetralogy: Meditation as Drama. NASEEB SHAHEEN: Deriving Adjectives from Nouns. TED R. SPIVEY: The Apocalyptic Symbolism of W. B. Yeats and T. S. Eliot. EDWARD STONE: The Other Sermon in 'Moby–Dick'. M. G. WILLIAMS: 'In Memoriam': A Broad Church Poem.

Volume 5. Amsterdam 1972. 236 p. Hfl. 40.–
PETER G. BEIDLER: Chaucer's Merchant and the Tale of January. ROBERT A. BRYAN: Poets, Poetry, and Mercury in Spenser's Prosopopia: Mother Hubberd's Tale. EDWARD M. HOLMES: Requiem For A Scarlet Nun. E. ANTHONY JAMES: Defoe's Narrative Artistry: Naming and Describing in Robinson Crusoe. MICHAEL J. KELLY: Coleridge's "Picture, or The Lover's Resolution": its Relationship to "Dejection" and its Sources in the Notebooks. EDWARD MARGOLIES: The Playwright and his Critics. MURRAY F. MARKLAND: The Task Set by Valor. RAYMOND S. NELSON: Back to Methuselah: Shaw's Modern Bible. THOMAS W. ROSS: Maimed Rites in Much Ado About Nothing. WILLIAM B. TOOLE: The Metaphor of Alchemy in Julius Caesar. PAUL WEST: Carlyle's Bravura Prophetics. GLENA D. WOOD: The Tragi-Comic Dimensions of Lear's Fool. H. ALAN WYCHERLEY: "Americana": The Mencken – Lorimer Feud.

Volume 6. Amsterdam 1972. 235 p. Hfl. 40.–
GEORG W. BOSWELL: Superstition and Belief in Faulkner. ALBERT COOK: Blake's Milton. MARSHA KINDER: The Improved Author's Farce: An Analysis of the 1734 Revisions. ABE LAUFE: What Makes Drama Run? (Introduction to Anatomy of a Hit). RICHARD L. LOUGHLIN: Laugh and Grow Wise with Oliver Goldsmith. EDWARD MARGOLIES: The American Detective Thriller & The Idea of Society. RAYMOND S. NELSON: Shaw's Heaven, Hell, and Redemption. HAROLD OREL: Is Patrick White's Voss the Real Leichhardt of Australia? LOUIS B. SALOMON: A Walk With Emerson On The Dark Side. H. GRANT SAMPSON: Structure in the Poetry of Thoreau. JAMES H. SIMS, Some Biblical Light on Shakespeare's Hamlet.

ROBERT F. WILLSON, Jr.: Lear's Auction. JAMES N. WISE: Emerson's "Experience" and "Sons and Lovers". JAMES D. YOUNG: Aims in Reader's Theatre.

Volume 7. Amsterdam 1973. 235 p. Hfl. 40.–
HANEY H. BELL Jr.: Sam Fathers and Ike McCaslin and the World in Which Ike Matures. SAMUEL IRVING BELLMAN: The Apocalypse in Literature. HALDEEN BRADDY: England and English before Alfred. DAVID R. CLARK: Robert Frost: "The Thatch" and "Directive". RALPH MAUD: Robert Crowley, Puritan Satirist. KATHARINE M. MORSBERGER: Hawthorne's "Borderland": The Locale of the Romance. ROBERT E. MORSBERGER: The Conspiracy of the Third International. "What is the metre of the dictionary?" – Dylan Thomas. RAYMOND PRESTON: Dr. Johnson and Aristotle. JOHN J. SEYDOW: The Sound of Passing Music: John Neal's Battle for American Literary Independence. JAMES H. SIMS: Enter Satan as Esau, Alone; Exit Satan as Belshazzar: *Paradise Lost*, BOOK (IV). MICHAEL WEST, Dryden and the Disintegration of Renaissance Heroic Ideals. RENATE C. WOLFF: Pamela as Myth and Dream.

Volume 8. Amsterdam 1973. 231 p. Hfl. 40.–
SAMUEL I. BELLMAN: Sleep, Pride, and Fantasy: Birth Traumas and Socio-Biologic Adaptation in the American-Jewish Novel. PETER BUITENHUIS: A Corresponding Fabric: The Urban World of Saul Bellow. DAVID R. CLARK: An Excursus upon the Criticism of Robert Frost's "Directive". FRANCIS GILLEN: Tennyson and the Human Norm: A Study of Hubris and Human Commitment in Three Poems by Tennyson. ROBERT R. HARSON: H. G. Wells: The Mordet Island Episode. JULIE B. KLEIN: The Art of Apology: "An Epistle to Dr. Arbuthnot" and "Verses on the Death of Dr. Swift". ROBERT E. MORSBERGER: The Movie Game in Who's Afraid of Virginia Woolf and The Boys in the Band. EDWIN MOSES: A Reading of "The Ancient Mariner". JOHN H. RANDALL: Romeo and Juliet in the New World. A Study in James, Wharton, and Fitzgerald "Fay ce que vouldras". JOHN E. SAVESON: Conrad as Moralist in Victory. ROBERT M. STROZIER: Politics, Stoicism, and the Development of Elizabethan Tragedy. LEWIS TURCO: Manoah Bodman: Poet of the Second Awakening.

Volume 9. Amsterdam 1973. 251 p. Hfl. 40.–
THOMAS E. BARDEN: Dryden's Aims in *Amphytryon*. SAMUEL IRVING BELLMAN: Marjorie Kinnan Rawling's Existentialist Nightmare *The Yearling*. SAMUEL IRVING BELLMAN: Writing Literature for Young People. Marjorie Kinnan Rawlings' "Secret River" of the Imagination. F. S. JANZOW: "Philadelphus," A New Essay by De Quincey. JACQUELINE KRUMP: Robert Browning's Palace of Art. ROBERT E. MORSBERGER: The Winning of Barbara Undershaft: Conversion by the Cannon Factory, or "Wot prawce selvytion nah?" DOUGLAS L. PETERSON: Tempest-Tossed Barks and Their Helmsmen in Several of Shakespeare's Plays. STANLEY POSS: Serial Form and Malamud's Schlemihls. SHERYL P. RUTLEDGE: Chaucer's Zodiac of Tales. CONSTANCE RUYS: John Pickering–Merchant Adventurer and Playwright. JAMES H. SIMS: Death in Poe's Poetry: Varia-

tions on a Theme. ROBERT A. SMITH: A Pioneer Black Writer and the Problems of Discrimination and Miscegenation. ALBERT J. SOLOMON: The Sound of Music in "Eveline": A Long Note on a Barrel-Organ. J. L. STYAN: Goldsmith's Comic Skills. ARLINE R. THORN: Shelley's *The Cenci* as Tragedy. E. THORN: James Joyce: Early Imitations of Structural Unity. LEWIS TURCO: The Poetry of Lewis Turco. An Interview by Gregory Fitzgerald and William Heyen.

New Series. Volume 1. Edited by James L. W. West III. Amsterdam 1974. 194 p. Hfl. 40.–
D. W. ROBERTSON, Jr.: Chaucer's Franklin and His Tale. CLARENCE H. MILLER and CARYL K. BERREY: The Structure of Integrity: The Cardinal Virtues in Donne's "Satyre III". F. SAMUEL JANZOW: The English Opium-Eater as Editor. VICTOR A. KRAMER: Premonition of Disaster: An Unpublished Section for Agee's *A Death in the Family*. GEORGE L. GECKLE: Poetic Justice and *Measure for Measure*. RODGER L. TARR: Thomas Carlyle's Growing Radicalism: The Social Context of *The French Revolution*. G. THOMAS TANSELLE: Philip Gaskell's *A New Introduction to Bibliography*. Review Essay. KATHERINE B. TROWER: Elizabeth D. Kirk's *The Dream Thought of Piers Plowman*. Review Essay. JAMES L. WEST III: Matthew J. Bruccoli's *F. Scott Fitzgerald a Descriptive Bibliography*. Review Essay. JAMES E. KIBLER: R. W. Stallman's *Stephen Crane: A Critical Bibliography*. Review. ROBERT P. MILLER: Jonathan Saville's *The Medieval Erotic Alba*. Review.

New Series. Volume 2. **THACKERY. Edited by Peter L. Shillingsburg.** Amsterdam 1974. 359 p. Hfl. 70.–
JOAN STEVENS: *Vanity Fair* and the London Skyline. JANE MILLGATE: History *versus* Fiction: Thackeray's Response to Macaulay. ANTHEA TRODD: Michael Angelo Titmarsh and the Knebworth Apollo. PATRICIA R. SWEENEY: Thackeray's Best Illustrator. JOAN STEVENS: Thackeray's Pictorial Capitals. ANTHONY BURTON: Thackeray's Collaborations with Cruikshank, Doyle, and Walker. JOHN SUTHERLAND: A *Vanity Fair* Mystery: The Delay in Publication. JOHN SUTHERLAND: Thackeray's Notebook for *Henry Esmond*. EDGAR F. HARDEN: The Growth of *The Virginians* as a Serial Novel: Parts 1–9. GERALD C. SORENSEN: Thackeray Texts and Bibliographical Scholarship. PETER L. SHILLINSBURG: Thackeray Texts: A Guide to Inexpensive Editions. RUTH apROBERTS: Thackeray Boom: A Review. JOSEPH E. BAKER: Reading Masterpieces in Isolation: Review. ROBERT A. COLBY and JOHN SUTHERLAND: Thackeray's Manuscripts: A Preliminary Census of Library Locations.

New Series. Volume 3. Edited by James L. W. West III. Amsterdam 1975. 184 p. Hfl. 40.–
SAMUEL J. ROGAL: Hurd's Editorial Criticism of Addison's Grammar and Usage. ROBERT P. MILLER: Constancy Humanized: Trivet's Constance and the Man of Law's Custance. WELDON THORNTON: Structure and Theme in Faulkner's *Go Down, Moses*. JAYNE K. KRIBBS: John Davis: A Man For His Time. STEPHEN E. MEATS: The Responsibilities of an Editor of Correspon-

dence. Review Essay. RODGER L. TARR: Carlyle and Dickens *or* Dickens and Carlyle. Review. CHAUNCEY WOOD: Courtly Lovers: An Unsentimental View. Review.

New Series. Volume 4. Edited by James L. W. West III. Amsterdam 1975. 179 p. Hfl. 40.–
JAMES L. W. WEST III: A Bibliographer's Interview with William Styron. J. TIMOTHY HOBBS: The Doctrine of Fair Use in the Law of Copyright. JUNE STEFFENSEN HAGEN: Tennyson's Revisions of the Last Stanza of "Audley Court". CLIFFORD CHALMERS HUFFMAN: *The Christmas Prince*: University and Popular Drama in the Age of Shakespeare. ROBERT L. OAKMAN: Textual Editing and the Computer. Review Essay. T.H. HOWARD-HILL: The Bard in Chains: *The Harvard Concordance to Shakespeare.* Review Essay. BRUCE HARKNESS: Conrad Computerized and Concordanced. Review Essay. MIRIAM J. SHILLINGSBURG: A Rose is a Four-Letter Word; or, The Machine Makes Another Concordance. Review Essay. RICHARD H. DAMMERS: Explicit Statement as Art. Review Essay. A. S. G. EDWARDS: Medieval Madness and Medieval Literature. Review Essay. NOEL POLK: Blotner's Faulkner. Review.

New Series. Volume 5–6. **GYASCUTUS. Studies in Antebellum Southern Humorous and Sporting Writing. Edited by James L. W. West III.** Amsterdam 1978.
NOEL POLK: The Blind Bull, Human Nature: Sut Lovingood and the Damned Human Race. HERBERT P. SHIPPEY: William Tappan Thompson as Playwright. LELAND H. COX, Jr.: Porter's Edition of *Instructions to Young Sportsmen.* ALAN GRIBBEN: Mark Twain Reads Longstreet's *Georgia Scenes.* T. B. THORPE's Far West Letters, ed. Leland H. Cox, Jr. An Unknown Tale by GEORGE WASHINGTON HARRIS ed. William Starr. JOHNSON JONES HOOPER's "The 'Frinnolygist' at Fault" ed. James L. W. West III. SOUTH CAROLINA WRITERS in the *Spirit of the Times* ed. Stephen E. Meats. A NEW MOCK SERMON ed. James L. W. West III. ANOTHER NEW MOCK SERMON ed. A. S. Wendel. The PORTER-HOOPER Correspondence ed. Edgar E. Thompson.

New Series. Volume 7. **SANFORD PINSKER: The Languages of Joseph Conrad.** Amsterdam 1978. 87 p. Hfl. 20.–
Table of Contents: Foreword. Introductory Language. The Language of the East. The Language of Narration. The Language of the Sea. The Language of Politics. *Victory* As Afterword.

New Series. Volume 8. **GARLAND CANNON: An Integrated Transformational Grammar of the English Language.** Amsterdam 1978. 315 p. Hfl. 60.–
Table of Contents: Preface. 1) A Child's Acquisition of His First Language. 2) Man's Use of Language. 3) Syntactic Component: Base Rules. 4) Syntactic Component: Lexicon. 5) Syntactic Component: Transformational Rules. 6) Semantic Component. 7) Phonological Component. 8) Man's Understanding of His Language. Appendix: the Sentence-Making Model. Bibliography. Index.

New Series: Volume 9. **GERALD LEVIN: Richardson the Novelist: The Psychological Patterns.** Amsterdam 1978. 172 p. Hfl. 30.–
Table of Contents: Preface. Chapter One. The Problem of Criticism. Chapter Two. "Conflicting Trends" in *Pamela.* Chapter Three. Lovelace's Dream. Chapter Four. The "Family Romance" of *Sir Charles Grandison.* Chapter Five. Richardson's Art. Chapter Six. Richardson and Lawrence: the Rhetoric of Concealment. Appendix. Freud's Theory of Masochism. Bibliography.

New Series: Volume 10. **WILLIAM F. HUTMACHER: Wynkyn de Worde and Chaucer's Canterbury Tales. A Transcription and Collation of the 1498 Edition with Caxton^2 from the General Prologue Through the Knights Tale.** Amsterdam 1978. 224 p. Hfl. 40,–
Table of Contents: Introduction. Wynkyn's Life and Works. Wynkyn De Word's Contribution to Printing. Significance of Wynkyn's *The Canterbury Tales*. Significance of Wynkyn's Order of the Tales. Scheme of the Order of *The Canterbury Tales*. Wynkyn's Variants from CX^2. Printer's Errors. Spelling. Omissions in Wynkyn's Edition. Additions in Wynkyn's Edition. Transpositions in Wynkyn's Edition. Miscellaneous Variants in the Reading. Bibliography. Explanation of the Scheme of the Transcription and Recording of the Variants. The Transcription and Collation.

New Series: Volume 11. **WILLIAM R. KLINK: S. N. Behrman: The Major Plays.** Amsterdam 1978. 272 p. Hfl. 45,–
Table of Contents: Introduction. *The Second Man. Brief Moment. Biography. Rain From Heaven. End of Summer. No Time for Comedy. The Talley Method. But For Whom Charlie.* Language. Conclusion. Bibliography.

New Series: Volume 12. **VALERIE BONITA GRAY: *Invisible Man's* Literary heritage: *Benito Cereno* and *Moby Dick*.** Amsterdam 1978. 145p. Hfl. 30,–
Table of Contents: Democracy: The Politics of "Affirming the Principle" and Celebrating the Individual. The Spectrum of Ambiguity: From Mask Wearing to Shape-shifting. Whiteness or Blackness: Which Casts the Shadow? Melville's and Ellison's Methodology: Bird Imagery and Whale and Circus Lore. Social Protest. Bibliography.

New Series: Volume 13. **VINCENT DIMARCO and LESLIE PERELMAN: The Middle English Letter of Alexander to Aristotle.** Amsterdam 1978. 194p. Hfl. 40,–

New Series: Volume 14. **JOHN W. CRAWFORD: Discourse: Essays on English and American Literature.** Amsterdam 1978. 200p. 40,–
Contents: Chaucer's Use of Sun Imagery. The Fire from Spenser's Dragon: "The Faerie Queene," I.xi. The Changing Renaissance World in Thomas Deloney's Fiction. Shakespeare's Falstaff: A Thrust at Platonism. The Religious Question in *Julius Caesar.* Teaching *Julius Caesar:* A Study in Poetic Persuasion. Shakespeare: A Lesson in Communications. Intuitive Knowledge in *Cymbeline*. White Witchcraft in Tudor-Stuart Drama. Another

Biblical Allusion in *Paradise Lost. Absalom and Achitophel;* and Milton's *Paradise Lost.* Asem-Goldsmith's Solution to Timon's Dilemma. Dr. Johnson: A Modern Example of Christian Constancy. A Unifying Element in Tennyson's *Maud.* Arnold's Relevancy to the Twentieth Century. Sophocles' Role in "Dover Beach". Lest We Forget, Lest We Forget: Kipling's Warning to Humanity. The Garden Imagery in *Great Expectations.* "Victorian" Women in *Barchester Towers.* Another Look at "Youth". Forster's "The Road from Colonus". Biblical Influences in *Cry, the Beloved Country.* Huxley's *Island:* A Contemporary *Utopia.* The Generation Gap in Literature. Bred and Bawn in a Briar Patch – Deception in the Making. Success and Failure in the Poetry of Edwin Arlington Robinson. Naturalistic Tendencies in *Spoon River Anthology.* Primitiveness in "The Bravest Boat". Theme of Suffering in "Sonny's Blues". Nabokov's "First Love". The Temper of Romanticism in *Travels with Charley.* Unrecognized Artists in American Literature: Chicano Renaissance.

New Series: Volume 15. **ROBERT F. WILLSON, JR.: Landmarks of Shakespeare Criticism.** Amsterdam 1979. 113p. 25,–
Contents: Introduction. Thomas Rymer: On *Othello* (1692). Nicholas Rowe: Preface (1709-14). Alexander Pope: Preface (1725). Lewis Theobald: Preface (1740). Samuel Johnson: Preface (1765). Richard Farmer: Essay on the Learning of Shakespeare (1767). Gotthold Lessing: On Ghosts (1769). Walter Whiter: On Hell and Night in *Macbeth* (1794). William Richardson: On the Faults of Shakespeare (1797). August Wilhelm von Schlegel: Lecture XXIII. Shakespeare (1809-11). Johann Wolfgang von Goethe: Shakespeare ad Infinitum (1812?). Samuel Taylor Coleridge: On Shakespeare as a Poet (1811-12). William Hazlitt: On Shakespeare and Milton (1818). Thomas de Quincey: On the Knocking at the Gate in *Macbeth* (1823). Thomas Carlyle: The Hero as a Poet (1841). Ivan Turgenev: Hamlet and Don Quixote: the Two Eternal Human Types (1860). Edward Dowden: Shakespeare's Portraiture of Women (1888). Walter Pater: Shakespeare's English Kings (1889). Bernard ten Brink: Shakespeare as a Comic Poet (1895). Richard Moulton: Supernatural Agency in the Moral World of Shakespeare (1903). Leo Tolstoy: Shakespeare and the Drama (1906). J.J. Jusserand: What to Expect of Shakespeare (1911-12). Sigmund Freud: On Lady Macbeth (1916). George Bernard Shaw: On Cutting Shakespear (1919). Edmund Blunden: Shakespeare's Significances (1929). Selected Bibliography.

New Series: Volume 16. **A.H. Qureshi: Edinburgh Review and Poetic Truth.** Amsterdam 1979. 61p. 15,–

New Series: Volume 17. **RAYMOND J.S. GRANT: Cambridge Corpus Christi College 41: The Loricas and the Missal.** Amsterdam 1979. 127p. 30,–
Contents: Chapter I: The Loricas of Corpus 41. Chapter II: Corpus 41 – An 11th-Century English Missal. Appendix: Latin Liturgical material contained in

the Margins of Cambridge, Corpus Christi College 41. Endnotes: Chapter I and Chapter II.

New Series: Volume 18. **CARLEE LIPPMAN: Lyrical Positivism.** Amsterdam 1979. 195p. 40,–
Contents: Chapter I: Some Tenets. Chapter II: The Rape of *The Rape of the Lock.* Chapter III: García Márquez' Language Laboratory. Chapter IV: The Syntax of Persuasion. Afterword. Bibliography.

New Series: Volume 19. **EVELYN A. HOVANEC: Henry James and Germany.** Amsterdam 1979. 149p. 30,–
Contents: Preface. Introduction. Chapter I: A Travel Sketch. Chapter II: The Analytic Tourist. Chapter III: Life Into Fiction. Chapter IV: Value, Inconsistency, and Resolution. Bibliography. Index.

New Series: Volume 20. **SANDY COHEN: Norman Mailer's Novels.** Amsterdam 1979. 133p. 25,–
Contents: Chapter One: Norman Mailer in Context. Chapter Two: The Naked and the Dead. Chapter Three: Barbary Shore. Chapter Four: The Deer Perk. Chapter Five: An American Dream. Chapter Six: History As Novel As History: Armies of the Night. Chapter Seven: Why Are We In Vietnam? A Novel. Chapter Eight: Marilyn. A Biographical Note.

New Series: Volume 21. **HANS BERTENS:** The Fiction of Paul Bowles. Amsterdam 1979. 260p. 50,–
Contents: Chapter One: Introduction. Chapter Two: The Sheltering Sky. Chapter Three: Let It Come Down. Chapter Four: The Spider's House. Chapter Five: Up Above the World. Chapter Six: The Stories. Chapter Seven: Conclusion. Selected Bibliography. Index.

New Series: Volume 22. **RICHARD MANLEY BLAU:** The Body Impolitic. Amsterdam 1979. 214p. 45,–
Contents: Preface. Chapter I. Typee: In Search of Plump Sphericity. Chapter II. White Jacket: To Scourge a Man that is a Roman. Chapter III. Moby-Dick: Beware of the Spinal Complaint. Chapter IV. Pierre: Let them look out for me now! Epilogue. Bibliography.

New Series: Volume 23. From Caxton to Beckett, Essays presented to W.H. Toppen on the occasion of his seventieth birthday, Edited by Jacques B.H. Alblas and Richard Todd. With a foreword by A.J. Fry. Amsterdam 1979. 133p. 30,–
Contents: List of Plates. Foreword. Acknowledgements. Hans H. Meier: Middle English Styles in Translation: A Note on *Everyman* and Caxton's *Reynard.* Richard Todd: The Passion Poems of George Herbert. Jacques B.H. Alblas: The Earliest Editions of *The Pilgrim's Progress* as Source Texts for the First Dutch Translation of Bunyan's Allegory. Peter J. de Voogd et al.: A Reading of William Hogarth's *Marriage à la Mode.* M. Buning: *Lessness* Magnified. A.J. Fry: On the Agonies of Elitism.

New Series: Volume 24. **CAROL JOHNSON**: The Disappearance of Literature. Amsterdam 1980. 123p. 25,–

Contents: Chapter One: The Disappearance of Literature. Chapter Two: Randall Jarrell and the Art of Self Defense. Chapter Three: Paul Valery: The Art of Concealment. Chapter Four: Hart Crane's Unimproved Infancy. Chapter Five: John Berryman: The Will to Exceed. Chapter Six: The Poetics of Disregard: Homage to Basil Bunting. Chapter Seven: The Translator as Poet. Chapter Eight: An Adjunct to the Poet's Dossier. Chapter Nine: The Consummation of Consciousness: The Poetry of Delmore Schwartz. Chapter Ten: Mrs. Wharton's Profession: The Reef. Reconnoitered. Chapter Eleven: Eça De Queiroz: The Arbitrations of Irony. Chapter Twelve: Nabokov's Ada: Word's End. Chapter Thirteen: Hysteria Naturalized.

Rodopi

Editions Rodopi N.V., Keizersgracht 302-304, Amsterdam, The Netherlands